Andrea, it has been a pleasure to share this time and space with you! All the best!

Master the Waves of Life.

BRETT WADE, PHD

Copyright © 2013 Brett Wade.

All rights reserved. No part of this book may be reproduced, stored, or transmitted by any means—whether auditory, graphic, mechanical, or electronic—without written permission of both publisher and author, except in the case of brief excerpts used in critical articles and reviews. Unauthorized reproduction of any part of this work is illegal and is punishable by law.

ISBN: 978-1-4834-0352-6 (sc)
ISBN: 978-1-4834-0351-9 (e)

Library of Congress Control Number: 2013915851

Because of the dynamic nature of the Internet, any web addresses or links contained in this book may have changed since publication and may no longer be valid. The views expressed in this work are solely those of the author and do not necessarily reflect the views of the publisher, and the publisher hereby disclaims any responsibility for them.

Any people depicted in stock imagery provided by BIGSTOCK are models, and such images are being used for illustrative purposes only. Certain stock imagery © BIGSTOCK.

Lulu Publishing Services rev. date: 09/05/2013

CONTACT

To contact Dr. Brett Wade about the Ekahi Method or to book him for a speaking engagement visit www.ekahimethod.com. To book an appointment for the Ekahi Health Centre, send an email to: drbrettwade@ekahimethod.com

CONTENTS

Preface ix
Acknowledgments xi
Foreword *By Gillian Laura Roberts* xiii
Introduction xix
Glossary xxiii

FOUNDATIONS OF THE EKAHI METHOD

    Chapter 1: Building a Wave 3
    Chapter 2: Dissecting a Wave 9
    Chapter 3: Waves Are Life 21

THE EKAHI METHOD

Part I: **Discover Your Base Frequency**
    Chapter 4: Finding Your Base Frequency 39
    Chapter 5: Understanding Your Base Frequency 51

Part II: **Sense External Frequencies**
    Chapter 6: Sensing Frequencies in Other People 67
    Chapter 7: What Is Electrosmog? 81
    Chapter 8: Effects of Electrosmog on Base
                       Frequency and Health 93

Part III: **Reset to Base Frequency**
    Chapter 9: Being Out of Base Frequency 113
    Chapter 10: Resetting to Base Frequency 125

Part IV: Frequency Tune for Success
    Chapter 11: What Is Frequency Tuning and Why Should We Do It? 139
    Chapter 12: Frequency Tuning for Public Relationships 149
    Chapter 13: Frequency Tuning for Personal Relationships 157
    Chapter 14: Decision Making and Developing Intuition 171

Part V: Nourish Your Body with Resonant Frequencies
    Chapter 15: Resonance with Food 187
    Chapter 16: Resonance with Music, Sounds, and Words 201
    Chapter 17: Resonance with Exercise 213
    Chapter 18: Resonance with the Environment and Sleep 221

HEALING WITH WAVES

    Chapter 19: Light Waves for Health 233
    Chapter 20: Healing with Electromagnetism and Ultrasound 243

Conclusion 251
    Master the Waves of Life 251
References 253
Index 267
About the Author 275

PREFACE

For most of my life, I have thought about how everything in life has a common thread. I always looked for the commonalities shared by seemingly disparate objects or people. I suppose this interest reflects the way I learn: by grouping similarities. As a physiotherapist, I was fascinated by how people with certain diseases have similar histories and demographics. I noticed more subtle similarities in people with chronic diseases, what could be described as similar energies. I also began to see that, after many years of practice, many of my patients had energies similar mine.

I went on to complete a master's degree with a focus on fibromyalgia. I was interested in this complicated disease due to its unclear etiology and the fact that those who suffer from it are a rather homogenous group. Eventually, I could recognize a person with fibromyalgia from a mile away. I continued to practice and I developed a caseload focusing almost exclusively on the treatment and evaluation of people with chronic diseases such as fibromyalgia and multiple sclerosis.

Wanting to further understand some of the possible etiologies of complex diseases, I completed a doctorate degree with a dissertation examining the possible role of the earth's magnetic field in multiple sclerosis. While my research did not suggest that magnetic field causes the disease, it did present a different possible cofactor in disease expression. I saw a common thread in all the disease's suggested variables, and proposed a unified theory of multiple sclerosis etiology.

With my research background, clinical experience, and natural ability to see commonalities in living things, I began to look at a much bigger unifying theory that applied to all of life. From my years of research into frequencies of static magnetic fields from the earth's field to electromagnetic radiation like wireless technology, I understood that all life—in fact, all matter—radiates electromagnetic waves. Yes, even humans! We are affected by incoming radiated waves not only from external sources like the sun, but also from ourselves; we create our own radiation in the form of heat and extremely low frequency radio waves.

Armed with this realization that we are all essentially invisible waves of varying frequencies, I began to comprehend why people with similar diseases appear to have similar energies. I also understood why the patients who had remained on my caseload for many years appeared to resonate with me. I also noticed that people whom I enjoyed spending time with were on the same wavelength as me, while other people seemed to really drain my energy and affect me in a negative way. Finally I was beginning to make sense of this invisible energy source. If a person really understood their own frequency or energy, they could learn which environments made them ill and which environments might make them healthy.

I now realize that, by becoming aware of the power of these waves of electromagnetic radiation, and by understanding the importance of frequencies, we can transform our lives. We can learn to heal ourselves, to find a life partner, to get a good career, to eat right, to exercise well, and more. We have only to learn about the power of the Ekahi Method and then to start using it. We must learn to ride the waves and with time and practice - *master the waves of life*!

ACKNOWLEDGMENTS

I am a big wave rider. I am speaking metaphorically, of course. Actually, I have trouble standing up on a surfboard on the little rollers off the shore of Waikiki. What I mean is that while I am a yellow base frequency, I am a big amplitude yellow. This is to say, that being in my presence is like riding a roller coaster. I am aware of the fact that in the journey of my life, I have scared the pants off some people. I hope that I have also positively amplified people, too. I thank God every day for my love, Siri, who tolerates the extremes of my yellow base frequency wave and has helped me to realize the Ekahi Method in a way that would never have been possible without her.

I dedicate this work to the children in my blended family: Annora, Daison, Leif, Erik, Astri, and Haakon. I hope this work inspires you to realize your own limitless potential and to use your amazing talents to make the world a better place. In fact, I know you will. You are the most amazing people I have ever met and I am a much better wave rider because of you.

I am extremely grateful to my mother, Carol. Mom, without you and your earnest desire to make our family strong, none of this would exist. I am also grateful to my father, who is also a big wave rider. Through my parents I have learned how to enjoy riding the waves.

Thank you to my students, patients, friends, and family, who were exposed to the development of my theories and the Ekahi Method.

You must have thought I had fallen off my wave and bumped my head! Thank you to those who assisted in the development of the frequency profile and the refinement of my theories. I could not have done it without you.

FOREWORD
By Gillian Laura Roberts

> *"The time is now for you to really live as you were meant to live."*

You are in for such a treat with this gem of a book!

Like all diamonds, *the Ekahi Method* reflects a beautiful spectrum of colours, inviting us in a unique and powerful way into a whole new world of possibility: one that opens up when we discover we all naturally vibrate on the continuum of light in a highly *personal* way. Even better, it masterfully guides us in learning HOW to fully embrace living from our own personal vibration, so we can truly thrive in every area of our life. Sounds good to me!

I had the great good fortune to hear Dr. Brett Wade present *the Ekahi Method* at a conference recently, and I immediately knew I had to learn more about the work of this extraordinarily creative and committed healer. A true Renaissance man, Dr. Brett is clearly in his element and vibrating in perfect alignment with *his* personal frequency (yellow). As a writer and healer myself (and a fellow yellow), I work in the realm of mind and heart, focusing on the power of our thoughts, feelings, and intuition to create our personal and collective experiences in life. I've been very aware of how thoughts and feelings have their own unique vibrations, and that when we can shift them (or choose different ones), new experiences result. When Dr. Brett revealed that each of us has our own natural frequency guiding our optimal expression across the board, I had to discover what it meant to become a wave master!

Dr. Brett made a key discovery—a thought that changed *his* life forever: everything is a **wave**! Thank goodness he did. His passion for waves forms the foundation for every aspect of his patient work, research, and daily life—as well as his vision for what's possible in my life and yours. There is something so captivating when someone delivers their gift to the world—the revelation of a meaningful simplicity that becomes the sacred portal to the divine complexities of the Universe and our lives. *The Ekahi Method* is Dr. Brett's gift to us! Now—are *you* ready to catch the wave?

If you are alive and breathing, it's fun to realize you're already living your life riding waves, in every moment. The questions then become, "What waves are you riding?" and "Is the ride making you happy or not?" Dr. Brett has the answer to why you may be experiencing life the way you are, and if you're not feeling in the groove, how to "catch" the best waves for your best life! This means optimal health and happiness, living in harmony with those around you. What's better than that?

Never before have I come across such a multi-dimensional treatment that provides insight into the nature of life as it is unfolding around us in such an accessible, comprehensive way: Dr. Brett illuminates the fascinating science of waves (yes, they are everywhere!) and then builds an elegant bridge to the real-life effects they have on realms as novel as interpersonal relationships or their connection with particular disease patterns around the world. Wow—when we tap into life at this basic level of animation, things get really exciting!

But at the heart of the matter is YOU—what is *your* personal wavelength? Dr. Brett gives you a special way to discover this for yourself and reveals specific characteristics of your wave group. Have you ever noticed you feel like eating every few hours…or maybe you're someone who forgets to eat for hours at a time? Do you prefer competitive sports or meditative yoga? Perhaps you like to wake up early, but run out of steam mid-afternoon while your best friend sleeps in, but gets energized later in the day. What begins to emerge in the pages of *the Ekahi Method* is a very interesting picture of how each group *prefers* to live—and the importance of knowing what it takes. All of the colours of the spectrum are beautiful, yet they are *different*—and that is good: when we are happy right down to our wavelength, anything is possible!

Dr. Brett deftly moves us into a place of integrating the awareness of our natural or "base frequency" into our consciousness of others' natural vibrations, teaching us how to interact in ways that engender connection and harmony. As harmony always breeds health, as a physiotherapist, Dr. Brett is careful to give us insights into how operating in our base frequency—and equally important, how to return to it when we pop out—allows us our greatest opportunity for holistic well-being. We are reminded of the importance of continually *tuning* our awareness to our base frequency—our natural wave expression—as well as *nourishing* ourselves in this authentic expression. Along the way, he makes all this information easily understandable, interesting, and entertaining by including further explanations ("In Dr. Brett's Words"), as well as case studies and important points to note, for readers of all colours.

What I love about Dr. Brett's work is his many gifts of distinction. His keen desire is for you to realize where you are similar to others and also to honour your precious uniqueness. I am also struck with how much heart Dr. Brett has infused into every step of this journey for you, his treasured reader. In the same way as he asks each of us to meet ourselves where we truly are, he meets his readers where they are—seemingly anticipating every question and lovingly providing resources to satisfy those who want to understand the scientific nature of waves and the Ekahi Method, as well as nurturing those who are simply seeking to understand more about who they are. For all of us, he provides a lovely array of not just educational insights, but practical applications for this knowledge, including key ways to support the transformation of information to personal wisdom. Living who we truly are makes us *really* vibrate!

As a meditation instructor myself, I was also so impressed to find him prescribing this powerful practice as a way to honour, embody, and re-calibrate ourselves to our base frequency. Though there may only be 5 colours, there are nearly 7 billion folks vibrating in their own unique way on the planet: we cannot help but affect one another, so it's key to know how to come home to ourselves. However, as Judge Thomas Troward also posited, "Where there is one point of consciousness, all of Consciousness is present." Indeed, we are One—*Ekahi*. You are an individualized wave, yet there is no separation between the wave and the whole ocean. Like the ocean, Life just wouldn't be the same without your unique wave expression. The bottom line is, there's simply no one like YOU.

The Ekahi Method is an opportunity to tap into this valuable understanding about yourself and the world around you. And you are in great hands, as you will find Dr. Brett genuinely cares about YOU—whether you are an audience member, reader, patient or someone half way around the world. I hope that by reading this magical book and practicing his loving instructions, you will find your wave is not only beautiful and perfectly you, but that you come to feel your part in a bigger whole—the one that is moving us all to a higher level of awareness and consciousness. That by *mastering the waves of life*—discovering your base frequency, honouring it, and learning how to resonate harmoniously with those around you—you will make every day the best ride of your life, and even help to transform the world!

> *"Once you learn to find and honor your rhythms,*
> *you will find success in all aspects of life.*
> *The time is now for you to really live*
> *as you were meant to live."*

Are you ready to catch *your* wave?

Gillian Laura Roberts, BSc., RScP.
Licensed Spiritual Practitioner, Teacher, Sacred Ceremony Officiant
Owner—Purepower Spiritual Coaching;
Co-Owner, The Thought Publications, Inc. & Co-creator of the bestselling book, *"The Thought That Changed My Life Forever"*
www.thethoughtpublications.com
www.ignitepurepower.com

August 3, 2013
Vancouver, BC

INTRODUCTION

Ekahi means "one" in Hawaiian.

This book is called the Ekahi Method, or the "one method", because there is one thing that connects all living and nonliving things: waves. Understanding the power of these waves, most of which are invisible, can help us understand how to maximize the positive effects of waves and minimize their negative effects on our health and happiness. Once we learn to *master the waves of life*, we can utilize their power to assist us with the big things in life: finding a compatible life partner, finding the right job, finding healthy ways of eating and exercising, finding happiness. It sounds too simple to be true, doesn't it? But the truth is that it *is* that simple. Some people deceive us into believing that if we keep our noses to the grindstone, don't ask questions, and follow their programs for weight loss, making money, finding happiness, or creating a successful relationship. In my experience, these programs rarely work in the long-term for anyone except the person peddling the program.

Self-help gurus love to provide people with steps to or formulas for success. Diet and exercise programs often ask people to follow complicated regimes designed for failure. These programs treat us as if we are all the same, though we most certainly are not. The Ekahi Method shows you that you have your own unique *base frequency*. As you honor your own waves and energy, you will learn what works best for you. It is time to stop following other people's formulas and steps to success. They may work for some, but most will fail. To be successful in life, we must each find a path that resonates with our base frequency.

The Ekahi Method will improve all aspects of your life by honoring your own natural frequency. You will find success with this method because you will be following a path you yourself have discovered and directed. The Ekahi Method uniquely uses scientific research and principles to explain its effects, which are real and quantifiable and have been researched, and tested. I do not consider the Ekahi Method to be a new age idea. In fact, it is simply a way of honoring the energy that is within you and that has been around since the universe formed. In other words, the Ekahi Method is *original* age.

You might wonder about my credentials on this subject. I write from my perspective as a scientist, health practitioner, and college professor. I have used this method successfully with my patients for many years. I know it works. Many self-help books and alternative therapies attempt to bend science to fit their therapies or philosophies because they actually have no logical explanations whatsoever. In writing this book, I wanted to make sure the Ekahi Method could be explained by science.

I guarantee that if you follow the Ekahi Method for six weeks, your life will change; you will never live the same way again. The beautiful part is that you only have to learn one thing. Once you learn to find and honor your rhythms, your base frequency, you will find success in all aspects of life. It is time for you to live as you were meant to live.

This book is divided into five parts and twenty chapters. The five parts of the Ekahi Method are the following:

1. Discover Your Base Frequency
2. Sense External Frequencies

3. Reset to Base Frequency
4. Tune Frequency for Success
5. Nourish with Resonant Frequencies

In addition, there are two bookends to the five parts. To begin, there is an introduction of three chapters: Building a Wave, Dissecting a Wave, and Waves Are Life. This introduction contains important information that sets the stage for the subsequent chapters. The final chapter of the book, Healing with Waves, discusses treatments that have been shown to be useful in healing and possibly preventing diseases and medical conditions ranging from cartilage injury to cancer. This chapter should not be skipped.

Throughout the book, you will find italicized sections which draw your attention to important concepts:

- Dr. Brett Says
- Case Study
- Important Point

At the end of each chapter is a summary of the most important concepts. It is important to read this book in a linear fashion. If you choose to skip sections, you may miss important information.

Please join me as we learn to master the waves of life.

GLOSSARY

The Ekahi Method employs some specific words and phrases. Some of those terms are listed below. While they are also defined within the text, this glossary helps set the stage for your introduction to the Ekahi Method.

ekahi: In Hawaiian, *ekahi* means "one." The one thing that is the central theme of the Ekahi Method is waves.

base frequency (also base frequency class or color): Your natural wave frequency. The Ekahi Method classifies people into: red, yellow, green, blue, and violet.

the frequency profile: The profile which you complete in chapter 4 assigns you a *base frequency* (see above). The profile combines two objective measurements: resting heart rate and respiratory rate and seven questions about your energy.

natural zone: The natural height of your waves when you feel at your best. It is a description of your energy when it is not too high and not too low.

wave amplifier: People or things that can push the range of your waves out of your *natural zone* to much higher extremes, from top to bottom.

wave reducers: People or things that can diminish the height of your waves below your *natural zone*.

frequency tuning: The deliberate act of temporarily matching someone else's base frequency in order to improve a situation between two people.

constructive interference (resonance): These scientific terms are used interchangeably to refer to the observation in physics that when waves of similar frequencies come together, they summate and get bigger. This effect raises your energy, acting like a *wave amplifier*.

destructive interference: The observation in physics that when two waves of very different frequencies come together, the wave energy flattens. This effect acts like a *wave reducer*.

frequency: The number of times a wave moves up and down (cycles) in a period of time—usually one second. Often measured in Hertz (Hz).

amplitude: The height of the wave. Used interchangeably with the word *energy* in the Ekahi Method.

Foundations of the Ekahi Method

CHAPTER 1

Building a Wave

When the student is ready, the master appears.
—Buddhist proverb

Waves are life. Anybody who has ever met me knows that once I get on the subject of waves, I can talk for hours. You might wonder how waves could be this exciting. But what is not to love? One of my favorite things to do is to watch the ocean waves. I have lived on the ocean for many years at different points in my life and I find myself extremely attracted to waves. The waves on the ocean are mechanical waves. In this book we will also learn about the incredible power of the subtle waves that travel through space, moving around us and, in some cases, right through us. These waves are known as electromagnetic waves.

My passion for understanding the power of electromagnetic waves actually began with my curiosity about the effects of meditation and the power of belief. Besides being curious about all things in life, I was also someone who needed constant dramatic change. Whenever I felt unhappy, I thought that I needed to make a change—a change of where I lived, a change of friends, a change of hobbies, or a change of career. I had the privilege of living in Hawaii and working as a physical therapist several years ago. While living and working in this paradise, I began to experience a prolonged unhappiness. I didn't understand what was causing it, but I decided that it must mean I needed to change my career.

I was certain this action would cure my depression. I focused all my efforts and daily meditations on making it happen. I took some courses at the local university and befriended a local naturopathic doctor. I followed the formula that had worked for me in the past: have a desire to make a change, immerse yourself in the process, and surround yourself with people who have the thing you want. I had learned this skill from years of practice and from reading hundreds of self-improvement books, and I became almost arrogant about my proficiency in it. It seemed I was able to literally create whatever I wanted.

My tactics once again proved successful. While still working full time as a physical therapist and taking courses in botany and organic chemistry in Hawaii, I applied to a naturopathic medical school in Arizona and was accepted. I was elated! Finally, I could move out of my depression and start doing something that would make me happy. I started to make preparations to wrap up my physical therapy work and leave Hawaii. A few weeks before I was set to leave for Arizona, I was strolling down a street when a sign in the window of an unremarkable building caught my eye. It read, "Spiritual Readings Available by Appointment." Even though I had found great successes with alternative practices such as meditation, and prayer, spiritual and psychic readings were not my thing. Ordinarily, I would have walked right by, but for some reason that day, I decided to enter the building.

I was greeted by a peaceful, slender man with facial hair and a ponytail, the kind of guy you might expect to be into new age practices. He shook my hand and asked me how he could help. I asked to make an appointment for a spiritual reading. He nodded and motioned me to the desk, which was adorned with the usual new age trimmings: incense, statues of Buddha, and Tibetan prayer flags. He wrote my name down in a book for an appointment two days later. I took a little card with my appointment time written on it and once again shook the man's hand. He smiled and said that he looked forward to seeing me.

When I walked out of the building I found myself asking, *Why did I go in there? Why would someone like me, who has never thought much about psychics, suddenly feel so compelled to have a spiritual reading?* I didn't even know what a spiritual reading was! Two days later, I returned to receive my reading. The peaceful man greeted me at the door and brought me back to the counter, where I paid fifty dollars. I was feeling nervous. He motioned me to take a seat in a chair in the middle of the room, and gracefully sat facing me in a chair a few feet away. He began by closing his eyes and meditating for what seemed an eternity. I thought perhaps I should close my eyes and try to meditate as well. This part of the process, at least, I was familiar with.

After about five minutes of quiet time, he let out little giggle and opened his eyes. With a wide smile, he said, "How can I help you?" This question caught me a bit off guard. I told him about my decision to leave my current profession and enter a naturopathic medical school. I explained how I had worried that I wasn't really helping people as much as I could be, and that I believed I would be much happier in a new career. After listening to me, he just sat there and smiled for what felt like ten minutes, but was probably only a few seconds. I was stunned. He said, "Why do you want to change careers?" I quickly replied, "I told you that I want to help people in a larger capacity." I was beginning to think this was the worst fifty bucks I had ever spent. Then he asked, "Why aren't you able to help people now?" I explained that as a physical therapist I felt I had a limited number of techniques, but as a naturopathic physician, I would have many more ways that I could help people. He listened intently, then took a deep breath and told me a story that would eventually change my life.

Brett Wade, PhD

Great Healers Sometimes Sell Ice Cream

He looked carefully into my eyes and said, "I want to tell you a story about the greatest healing experience I ever had. It happened a few years ago while I was buying ice cream at a local ice cream shop." I tried my best not to let my mind wander as he began.

"I recall waking up in the morning and not feeling particularly well. I don't know why, but I felt depressed and tired for no particular reason. I went through my usual routine in the morning as I readied myself for work, but I couldn't shake the depressed feeling. I didn't start work until noon that day, so before I went into the office I decided, for some reason, to stop and get some ice cream. I parked my car and proceeded to the ice cream shop. It was an overcast day, so the shop was not particularly busy. There was an elderly couple sitting at a table enjoying a sundae.

As I tried to decide what type of ice cream I wanted, a young girl approached the counter from the back. She began to smile, and I honestly can't remember having ever seen such a beautiful smile. She was radiant. In that moment, which seemed to last several minutes but was probably only a few seconds, she uttered five simple words that changed my day: "How can I help you?" These words were exactly what I needed to hear. This young girl didn't know it but she reached out and touched me in ways and with power that she, herself, was likely unaware she even possessed. After serving my ice cream, I paid her and in an almost trance like state I sat down in shock at the way this girl had completely changed my mood and altered my physiology. I was inexplicably happy, optimistic, and relaxed. I finished my ice cream, and before I left the shop, I scribbled a note on a napkin. I simply wrote, "Thank you for making my day better—you are a great healer." As I stood up to take my garbage and put it in the trash, I handed the Ice Cream Healer the napkin, smiled and said "goodbye." This day, which started out to be a very sad day, turned out to be one of the greatest days in a long time.

Okay, I could see how the story moved him but I failed to see what this had to do with me! He went on to explain that I "shouldn't be fooled by disguises and sometimes great healers do indeed sell ice cream." Okay, maybe I could buy the idea that this girl was gifted at healing. Why not? I said to him, "Why wouldn't she want to use that talent in a bigger way?" He quickly replied, "Why does she need to do it *bigger*? What if this girl is truly happy and sees that through her simple act of service, she makes others happy? She was making minimum wage, but she appeared to be much happier than you. You can see that exchanging a white lab coat for the uniform of an ice-cream-shop employee does not necessarily mean increased happiness."

He went on to ask, "What is it that you really want?" He explained that if we acknowledge that in every job involves helping people, then there must be something deeper that I desired. Then I was overcome by emotion. Tears streamed down my cheeks as I stared at the floor. I composed myself and said, "I want to be happy." He smiled again and nodded. "Exactly. You are already helping others. You need to find and experience inner peace and happiness for yourself. You might experience this right now in your career as a physical therapist, or you might experience it as a naturopathic physician, but you are no less likely to experience happiness serving ice cream."

At the end of my reading, I felt completely different. I felt stripped down naked to my core and much lighter. I bid farewell to my spiritual reader and headed out the door. I felt the warm tropical breeze on my skin. I smelled gardenias in the air and could hear the ocean waves crashing against the black rock. My senses were acute and I actually felt happy. I walked home slowly and sat in my house feeling genuinely happy. I had gained a completely new direction in my life.

I wanted to understand how we communicate and understand other people without words. I wanted to understand invisible forces and how we can use them to heal ourselves and others.

Since plans were already in motion for me to leave the island, I packed my bags and boarded a plane—back home, to Canada. I landed without the slightest idea of where my life was going to take me now, but I knew that my old pattern of forcing a plan into action would not do. Instead, I would start listening and paying attention to the natural rhythms of life. I would realize that happiness did not come from a specific career, but from environments, both internal and external. I would dedicate myself to understanding how subtle forces in our environments affect us in profound ways. I would practice meditation regularly, and I would one day write about this experience.

Fast forward to fifteen years after that fateful spiritual reading in Hawaii. I am now mastering the waves of life. There have been spills and crashes along the way and I expect that to continue, but I have finally learned the lesson that life can be an amazing ride if we learn but one thing. Once we understand the power of the Ekahi Method—the power of waves—we can use it to our full advantage and make positive changes in our lives. Join me in learning to become aware of this energy and make use of its power, in finding the *natural zone* of your wave, your *base frequency*. We will together learn to ride the waves of life and soon master the waves of life!

CHAPTER 2

Dissecting a Wave

God runs electromagnetics by wave theory on Monday, Wednesday, and Friday, and the Devil runs them by quantum theory on Tuesday, Thursday, and Saturday.
—*William Bragg*

There are two types of waves: *mechanical* and *electromagnetic*. Believe it or not, you are already familiar with both types—at least, with certain frequencies and intensities (which will be defined later) of these waves. The Ekahi Method will teach you about mechanical and electromagnetic waves and their dramatic impact on our lives. You will learn that some waves can be good for us and are, in fact, vital, while other waves can literally kill us.

If you have ever been pushed down by a wave in the ocean or watched the devastating effects of a tsunami, you know how powerful mechanical waves can be. If you have ever seen a laser cut through steel or watched a microwave oven melt a pizza in seconds, you have witnessed the power of electromagnetic radiation waves. In this chapter we will explore these two types of waves as we build knowledge before learning to apply the Ekahi Method.

Table 1. Examples of Mechanical and Electromagnetic Waves

Mechanical Waves	Electromagnetic Waves
Guitar string vibrating	Ultraviolet radiation
Sound waves	Visible light waves
Seismic waves from earthquake	Infrared radiation
Waves on water	Microwaves
Ultrasound or sonar	X-rays

Dr. Brett Says

- It may be tempting to skip past some of the descriptions and theory of electromagnetic radiation, but unless you already have an understanding of this force, I urge you to stick with reading this basic information. I promise to do my best to make understanding this fundamental force of life interesting!

Four fundamental forces, also known as interactive forces, govern the way particles interact with each other. You will already be very familiar with one of these forces: gravity. The other three are weak forces, strong forces, and electromagnetic forces. You may have heard of the superstring theory. It is a theory which attempts to explain how these four forces relate to each other and interact with all matter in the universe. This theory is involves minute vibrations (waves) connecting all of life together. Without question, all four of the forces are important to us, but for the purposes of understanding and applying the Ekahi Method, we need to focus on electromagnetic force and its waves and, of course, mechanical waves such as sound waves.

Table 2. Four Fundamental Forces in Nature

Force	Example
Gravitational	Attractive force between objects
Weak	Radioactive decay
Strong	Holds nucleus of atoms together
Electromagnetic	Attractive or repulsive forces between objects/particles.

Electromagnetic radiation may at first sound like a scary thing, but most radiation is invisible and harmless. Electromagnetic radiation is invisible waves emitted by moving charged particles. The best example of a source of electromagnetic radiation is our sun. The sun emits electromagnetic radiation of almost infinite different frequencies. We therefore classify these different frequencies as a spectrum which ranges from the very lowest frequency to the very highest (see figure 1).

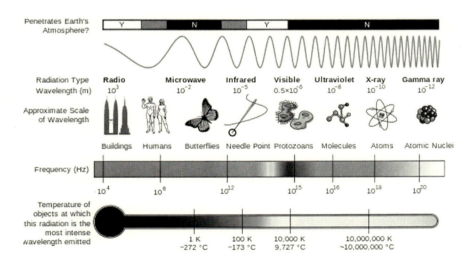

Figure 1. Electromagnetic Spectrum
By Inductiveload, NASA [GFDL (http://www.gnu.org/copyleft/fdl.html) or CC-BY-SA-3.0 (http://creativecommons.org/licenses/by-sa/3.0/)], via Wikimedia Commons

It is at this point that I need to emphasize some definitions for words that I will be using regularly in this book. Let's start with the word *frequency*. Frequency is simply the number of times a wave cycles (moves from bottom to top to bottom) in a second (figure 2). We describe the frequency of waves as the number of cycles per second—or Hertz, after Heinrich Hertz, one of the early pioneers of electromagnetic theory. Another aspect of waves we need to understand is that when the wave frequency is low, the wavelength is long, and when the frequency is high, the wavelength is short; it is an inverse relationship. The height of a wave is known as the *amplitude*. Think about turning the volume up on a stereo: this increases the amplitude of the sound wave.

Sine Wave

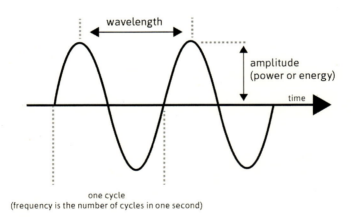

Figure 2. Waves (Frequency, Intensity, and Wavelength)
Created by Chris Arlidge, Media Button (2013)

Dr. Brett Says

- It may be hard to believe, but all of life is affected by waves. Waves, whether electromagnetic or mechanical, have two main parts: frequency (number of waves in a second) and amplitude (height of the wave). In the Ekahi Method, you will discover your own base frequency. It represents the rate at which you make your waves. Amplitude is essentially the height of your waves. Some days, your waves will be big (extremes of high and low energy), and other days, your waves will be much smaller (low energy). It is important to remember that no matter how big your waves on any given day, you will always cycle up and down in energy.

In the glossary, I introduced two terms that we use regularly to describe interacting waves: *constructive interference* and *destructive interference*. Interference occurs when two waves meet to together form one resulting wave. As shown in figure 3, constructive interference (top picture) is the physical effect in which two waves (electromagnetic or mechanical) come together and summate, or add up, to create a higher amplitude. Destructive interference (bottom picture) occurs when two waves of different frequencies meet and flatten out.

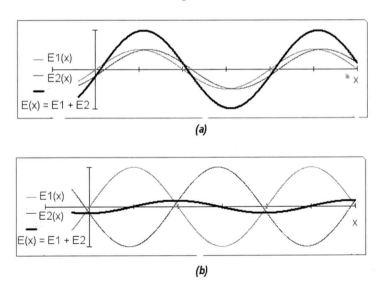

Figure 3. Constructive (a) and Destructive Interference (b)
By KaWus1093 (Own work) [CC-BY-SA-3.0 (http://creativecommons.org/licenses/by-sa/3.0) or GFDL (http://www.gnu.org/copyleft/fdl.html)], via Wikimedia Commons

Brett Wade, PhD

Dr. Brett Says

- In chapter 5 you are going to learn about how some people and environments have frequencies of destructive interference. We call these people or environments that flatten our waves wave reducers. We will also learn that the people and environments that cause constructive interference are wave amplifiers. It is normal for our energies to go up and down with our waves throughout the course of a day. Sometimes there are uncontrollable wave reducers and wave amplifiers that can make our waves fluctuate at rates unnatural to us; they can actually pull us out of our natural base frequency (chapter 4). But if all goes well, a normal day finds us riding our waves up and down, enjoying the peaks and troughs of the wave but savoring that amplitude of energy that is natural for us: the natural zone.

The essence of this book can be distilled to one thing; the Ekahi Method is about the power of waves. As mentioned, there are two types of waves: mechanical and electromagnetic. Most people are familiar with mechanical waves. These are waves on an ocean or lake, or sound waves, which nearly everybody has experienced. Mechanical waves differ from electromagnetic waves in that a medium such as water or air is required to transfer the wave energy. Electromagnetic waves do not require any medium to travel; they can travel in a vacuum, which is space without matter.

Most of us can think of examples of how mechanical waves affect us. Has your mood or energy (amplitude) ever been affected by music? How does the sound of waves lapping at the shore of a sandy beach make you feel? Electromagnetic waves, for the most part, have much more subtle effects. If we take another look at the electromagnetic spectrum (figure 4), we can see that it is divided up into ionizing and nonionizing radiation.

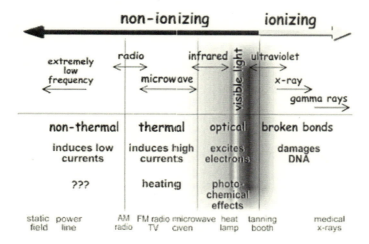

Figure 4. Ionizing vs. Non Ionizing Radiation
By Glenna Shields (www.epa.gov) [Public domain], via Wikimedia Commons

The part of the electromagnetic radiation that most people are familiar with is visible light. Our eyes, specifically the retina, have evolved to be able to detect specific frequencies of this electromagnetic radiation, thus permitting us to see color and light. In figure 4, notice that on the electromagnetic spectrum, visible light, the only light we can see, comprises only a very small section of the spectrum. We can use our other senses to pick up sensations such as heat, which is infrared radiation from sources such as the sun or other people.

Important Point

- The majority of the waves we interact with are completely invisible. While visible light and sound waves are the waves we are most conscious of, it is invisible waves, which have more subtle effects, that we must learn to feel.

Referring to figure 4 again, we can see that all forms of electromagnetic radiation are classified as either ionizing or nonionizing radiation.

Ionizing means that there is enough energy in the wave to tear apart parts of atoms or molecules. The dividing line between ionizing and non-ionizing radiation is ultraviolet radiation. Most people are familiar with ultraviolet (UV) as the invisible light that causes skin to tan (or burn). UV light is generally broken down into 3 sub-parts: A (longer wave length), B, and C (shortest and most energy). Most sunscreen is designed to limit UV-B exposure. UV-B has the perfect frequency to stimulate our skin cells to produce melanin—a pigment that darkens our skin to protect us from future exposures.

Looking again at the electromagnetic spectrum above (to the right in Figure 4) Ultraviolet B has the ability to be ionizing and therefore damage atoms or molecules in humans (and animals too). You may remember that an atom such as oxygen has small little particles called electrons whirling around its nucleus (Figure 5). It is these electrons that ionizing radiation can knock out of orbit. If this happens, we have the creation of a free radical. This means that the more UV-B exposure—the more free radicals are produced.

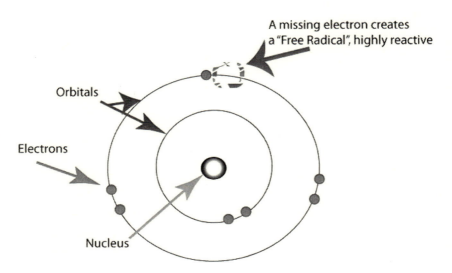

Figure 5. Oxygen Atom Losing Electron to Become a Free Radical
By Healthvalue (Own work) [CC-BY-SA-3.0 (http://creativecommons.org/licenses/by-sa/3.0)], via Wikimedia Commons

A free radical is a new atom or molecule created by the loss of an electron. The problem is that this creates a very reactive atom or molecule is very reactive; it can destabilize other molecules, including deoxyribonucleic acid (DNA), which contains the genes for repairing and recreating our cells. While free radicals might seem bad, they are produced naturally all the time. The most common free radicals produced in our bodies are oxygen free-radicals. This is an oxygen atom that has lost an electron as a result of a normal chemical reaction (figure 5). Fortunately, our body has natural *antioxidants* to neutralize the effects of free radicals. The real harm comes when one has an abundance of free radicals in the system. When the antioxidants can't keep up neutralizing the oxygen free-radicals, a process of disease could start.

Important Point

- One of the main reasons people recommend increasing fruits and vegetables in one's diet is that these foods have high antioxidant concentration.

Dr. Brett Says

- While free radicals are completely normal and, in fact, necessary to life, some environments and lifestyles can increase the levels of free radicals in the body, which can then lead to disease. We will learn more about free radicals in future chapters. Ekahi health consultants focus on prescribing diets and supplements to deal with excess free radical formation. They also make recommendations on environments which should be avoided because they may increase free radical production.

Fortunately, most sources of ionizing radiation are either filtered by the earth's magnetic field or easily shielded. Sources of excess ionizing radiation, such as X-rays, or radioactive material, such as uranium, can be avoided. Nonionizing radiation (left hand side of ultraviolet radiation in figure 4) is harder to avoid. While it is impossible to avoid exposure from some sources of nonionizing radiation like radio waves, in general, they do not cause us much harm. Since things like radio waves, infrared light, visible light, and microwaves are nonionizing, they likely have a less significant effect in creating free radicals.

Just because nonionizing radiation is subtle—in fact, nonionizing radiation passes right through us all the time—does not mean that it does not affect us. Chapter 7 will explore the potential negative side of chronic exposure to electromagnetic fields from man-made sources. A new term used to describe an environment that is essentially a soup of nonionizing radiation from man-made sources and of wide-ranging frequencies and intensities is *electrosmog*. Electrosmog and its potential health effects are explored further in chapter 7.

Important Point

- The lower the frequency of a wave, the more easily the wave will pass right through humans and even concrete. Radio waves, a type of extremely low frequency (ELF) wave, pass through us much more easily than ultraviolet waves, which are higher in frequency.

The Ekahi Method teaches you not only to determine your own base frequency and the frequency of others (nonionizing, by the way), but also how other parts of the nonionizing radiation spectrum and mechanical waves (chapters 19 and 20) can be used for balancing health and treating disease. We will explore in later chapters the importance of surrounding ourselves with resonant environments by considering the frequency of food, sounds, exercise, and environment. A resonant environment matches your frequency and helps you settle your waves into your natural zone.

In Summary

- There are two types of waves: electromagnetic and mechanical.
- Waves have both *frequency* (the number of waves in a second) and *amplitude* (the height of the wave).
- Both types of waves can be generated by humans and affect humans.
- Electromagnetic waves can be ionizing or nonionizing.
- Nonionizing radiation is all around us, and at low frequencies it can pass easily through us and through concrete walls.
- When two waves of similar frequencies interact, they can summate and increase in amplitude: *constructive interference*.
- When two waves of dissimilar frequencies interact, the wave can be flattened (decreased amplitude): *destructive interference*.
- People or things that decrease your energy (amplitude) have a very different frequency from yours and are called *wave reducers*. People or things that raise your energy are *wave amplifiers*.
- You want to find the right environments and the right people to help you find your *natural zone*, where you feel not too high and not too low.

CHAPTER 3

Waves Are Life

I'm surfing the giant life wave.
—William Shatner

In chapter 1, we learned that the Ekahi Method is about one thing: waves. We now need to appreciate that the Ekahi Method is not to be underestimated in its power to affect change; waves have significant power. Once we learn to *master the waves of life*, we can take full advantage of this power and use it to make our lives to healthier and happier.

Waves are the essence of life. Let's think about the waves that the human body produces. As I described in chapter 1, there are two types of waves: mechanical and electromagnetic. While much of the Ekahi Method focuses on invisible, nonionizing electromagnetic waves, it is important to note that mechanical waves are also very much a part of human life and the Ekahi Method. The gastrointestinal tract digests food and moves in a very wavelike motion. If you have ever seen a video of a beating heart, you will have noticed that it beats very much like a wave. The top half of the heart contracts, then just as it begins to relax, the bottom half of the heart contracts. This wave repeats itself. Sound is a mechanical wave. As we will see in chapter 16, it can have a tremendous effect on our *base frequency*.

Electromagnetic waves are not just external forces upon our bodies; we actually produce measurable electromagnetic waves of many different frequencies as well. The brain is a very active organ. From the time it begins to form in utero to the time we die, the brain is constantly using massive amounts of energy in the form of glucose (sugar) to work. In fact, the end of life is usually defined medically as the cessation of brain waves. The essential work that a brain does is to receive process reports and send information. The information that the brain relays is an electrical impulse that sent from a specific region of the brain down axons (parts of nerve cells) to a specific region of the spinal cord, which once again relays the impulse to a another tissue, such as a muscle or organ. All this activity in the brain gobbles up approximately 20 to 25 percent of our basal metabolic needs. Even at rest, we are using a tremendous amount of energy. In fact, the brain produces enough power to light a low-wattage light bulb!

This brain activity is a moving electrical charge. As we learned in chapter 1, a moving electrical charge creates an electric and a magnetic field and, therefore, an electromagnetic wave. The number of times this resultant electromagnetic wave propagates per second can be easily measured. This is the frequency (measured in Hz) of the nerve. It can be measured by placing sensors around the head; signals picked up by the sensors are relayed to a computer, which analyzes them and produces a graph (figure 6).

The following brain waves have been identified:

- (0-4 Hz) *Delta waves* are the lowest in frequency but highest in amplitude. They are generated by deep meditation and dreamless sleep. In addition, certain frequencies within the delta range trigger the release of a growth hormone which is beneficial for healing and regeneration.
- (4-7 Hz) *Theta waves* are associated with sleep and deep relaxation.

- (8-13 Hz) *Alpha waves* occur when we are relaxed and calm.
- (13-38 Hz) *Beta waves* occur when we are actively thinking and problem-solving.
- (30-100 Hz) *Gamma waves* occur during complex coordinated activities of the brain. Tibetan monks seem particularly skilled at reaching higher frequencies.

Important Point

- Remember that *frequency* is the number of times a wave moves up and down in a second and that it is measured in Hertz (Hz), or cycles per second (cps). The electricity flowing through the wires in your house travels at 60 Hz.

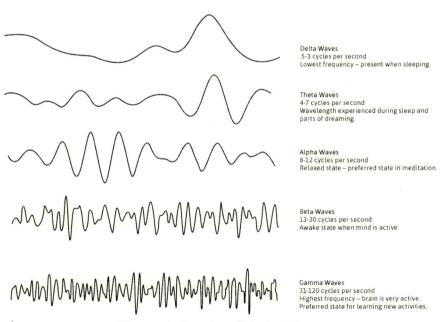

Figure 6. Graphs of Brain Waves
Created by Chris Arlidge, Media Button (2013)

Recall that an electromagnetic wave is produced by a moving electrical charge (in this case an ion such as sodium or potassium). In a wire carrying electricity, this charge is created by the transfer of a copper electron. So what do these measurable, unique waves tell us? First, they are evidence that we do emit an electromagnetic field from our brains. It is important to note that we do not necessarily spend long periods of time emitting any one brain wave, but move between the wave types regularly. It is not just our brains that emit this type of extremely low frequency (ELF) radiation (3-300 Hz); all nerves and muscles are capable of emitting ELF waves. Even the movement of free ions such as sodium, potassium, and calcium generates a magnetic field. So we are, in essence, electromagnetic beings that both produce electromagnetic waves and respond to them.

Dr. Brett Says

- It is irrefutable that humans produce electricity. Electric currents are produced from the movement of ions such as sodium and potassium back and forth across membranes in cells. This electrical current is easily measured. Not only active cells have a fluctuating voltage and current; all cells which contain ions in different concentrations will have a measurable voltage.

Important Point

- *Extremely low frequency (ELF)* waves are mentioned regularly in this book. Keep in mind that ELF is just a range defining waves that have a frequency less than 300 Hz. This is the range that easily passes through humans and, in fact, one of the frequency ranges produced by humans. Your household electricity at 60 Hz is in the ELF range.

- *Ultra high frequency (UHF)* is another range of waves mentioned regularly in the Ekahi Method. UHF range from three hundred million Hz to three billion Hz. These waves are not produced by humans, but their frequency is still low enough to penetrate human tissue. Examples of UHF are wireless communication signals from things like cellular telephones, wireless routers, cordless phones, and baby monitors.

In figure 7, we can see that it is the movement of charged particles such as sodium and potassium ions (Na^+ and K^+) that generates an electrical signal. These ions move back and forth across the membrane of cells like neurons to create this electrical charge.

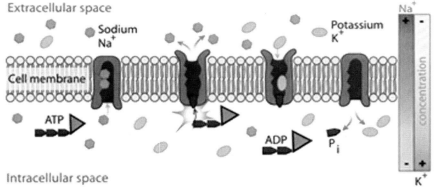

Figure 7. Movement of Sodium and Potassium across a Cell Membrane
By Lady of Hats Mariana Ruiz Villarreal [Public domain], via Wikimedia Commons

So what is so special about these ions? The reason they are able to generate an electrical signal is that each ion has its own electrical charge. Sodium and potassium have positive charges. Other ions such as chlorine (Cl^-) have a negative charge. Some cells in the body are *excitable*. This means that they are capable of producing and reacting to electrical charges. Nerve cells fit in this category, as do muscles. A signal may originate in the cell body of the neuron and then spread down the long tail-like section known as the axon. The axon has membranes around it capable of controlling the movement of the ions. As ions move back and forth across this membrane, an electrical charge is generated; it spreads down the axon, not unlike electricity moving along a copper wire.

We have learned that the brain is a major producer of extremely low frequency (ELF) waves in humans, but that it is not the only source. The heart is also a significant source of ELF waves. The heart rate of a person at rest is approximately 60 to 70 bpm (beats per minute). The heart contracts spontaneously through a discharge of nerves that originate in the atria, the upper chambers of the heart. This bundle of nerve cell bodies known as the sinoatrial node sends an electrical signal, or depolarizes, at a frequency that is genetically set for you. While diseases such as atherosclerosis, hypertension, and some chronic lung diseases can increase our resting heart rate, our heart rate at rest generally always returns to its base level.

The next chapter will instruct you to measure your resting heart rate and explain why this skill is a critical part of the Ekahi Method. As proof that there is electrical activity emanating from the heart, one need merely put a wireless transmitting heart rate monitor over the chest; this device will measure the electrical discharges from the sinoatrial node and the resultant depolarization of nerves leaving the sinoatrial node as they spread out along the bottom chambers of the heart. You may have seen graphs showing the electrical activity of the heart from an electrocardiogram (EKG). These waves have sharp points on them as opposed to the smooth curves of a sine wave. Nonetheless, it is still a wave.

The other excitable cells are in muscles. Not only do muscles have a rich supply of nerves, they are also a storehouse for ions such as calcium. When a muscle contracts, an electrical signal traveling along an axon stimulates the muscle. Calcium also floods through the muscle to facilitate the contraction. All this electrical activity is also a form of ELF wave and, like brain waves or heart muscle depolarization, muscle contractions can easily be measured. Surface electrodes placed on the skin can pick up the electricity generated by the movement of ions and assessed them using electromyography (EMG).

In chapter 1 we learned that, in addition to ELF waves, human beings emit infrared radiation and visible light. Much like the sun, most of the nonionizing radiation we emit is infrared radiation. Infrared radiation is produced when the body produces heat. The body converts thermal energy into electromagnetic radiation by emitting photons, which have wavelengths and frequencies in the far infrared spectrum of infrared radiation. All matter with a temperature greater than -273 °C (or 0 K) emits infrared and visible light. We can measure infrared radiation simply by assessing temperature.

Important Point

- Infrared radiation is also easily measured. The temperature of a person indicates the amount of energy they are releasing.

In my years of evaluating and treating patients I have determined that some people have higher energies (high frequency and high amplitude) than others. You, too, will surely have noticed this around high-energy people. This is not just a figure of speech—these people literally emanate high levels of nonionizing radiation. This high energy affects their muscle tone, the way they talk, the way they walk, their metabolisms, their jobs, the friends they associate with, and their partners.

Although it is difficult to assign an actual, quantifiable frequency to a person, some people have suggested that the base frequency of humans is approximately 70 to 79 Hz. I do not believe it to possible to reduce all humans, or any other matter, to one base frequency as it is difficult to sort out the influence of the many sources of internal nonionizing radiation, not to mention the external sources of nonionizing radiation. Recent research (Kim et al., 2002) attempting to quantify radiation emanating from humans is focused on measuring the frequency of low-energy photons called biophotons produced by all living cells. These biophotons are emitted at the far end of the visible light spectrum and extend into the ultraviolet spectrum. It seems that through our natural metabolic process of producing energy, we emit photons in this spectrum.

So far, we have learned that all humans—in fact, all matter—is capable of emitting waves of different frequencies. We emit mechanical waves via sounds and we emit many different types of nonionizing, electromagnetic radiation. The Ekahi Method teaches you that we actually communicate with each other nonverbally using these waves. Most of this communication occurs on an unconscious level. The Ekahi Method will also show you that by learning to respect your own natural frequency (*base frequency class*), you will learn how to adjust your frequency as needed and to sense frequencies emitted from other things, such plants and animals.

Dr. Brett Says

- Our cells emit a magnetic field of extremely low frequency. We emit biophotons in the ultraviolet range, we emit infrared radiation, we reflect visible light, and we produce audible sound waves. Even more fascinating is the fact that we regularly emit ionizing radiation in the form of gamma rays from radioactive sources within us! A human being is clearly an energetic mass emitting a wide range of ionizing and nonionizing wave frequencies, not unlike our very own sun.

I have already introduced the terms *wave reducers* and *wave amplifiers*. Now you know that they are an actual effect in physics that occurs

The Ekahi Method

when things or people with different frequencies (wave reducers) or similar frequencies (wave amplifiers) meet. The following image will help you understand how this effect might actually look if we were able to see the radiating waves between people.

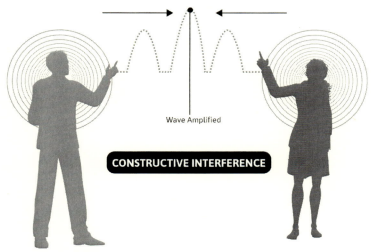

Figure 8. Constructive Interference (Wave Amplifier) Between People
Created by Chris Arlidge, Media Button (2013)

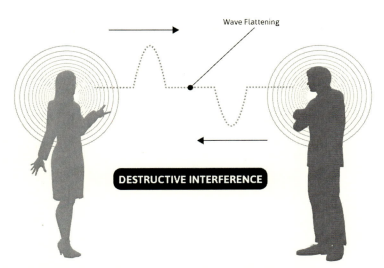

Figure 9. Destructive Interference (Wave Reducer) Between People
Created by Chris Arlidge, Media Button (2013)

We have all felt constructive interference (figure 8) when around somebody who makes us feel more energized. We often say things like, "I really resonate with that person," or "We are on the same wavelength." It seems these colloquialisms may have a grounding in science. When surrounded by people who emit similar frequencies to our own, we may actually experience an increase in our own waves due to resonance. These people are our wave amplifiers. Conversely, we have all been around people who have dissimilar frequencies to ours; being in their company actually brings us down. Our waves literally become flattened through destructive interference (figure 9). These people are our wave reducers.

This is the power of the Ekahi Method. You will learn to measure your own base frequency and start becoming aware of who or what your wave reducers and wave amplifiers are. Of course, we cannot avoid being surrounded by environments and people that lower our energy. The Ekahi Method will teach you ways to rejuvenate and reset your own base frequency. You will learn that no one color is more important than another, and that whatever your base frequency color is, you must respect and nourish it. This will lead to drastically improved health, happiness, and interpersonal relationships.

The environment in which we live is a soup of different frequencies of nonionizing radiation and of sound. These waves either pass right through us or bounce off of us; we barely notice them. Sometimes, mechanical sound waves affect us in positive or negative ways. Certain music played at certain times of the day can be incredibly soothing. Other kinds of music played at certain times of the day can be incredibly irritating. These are also examples of constructive or destructive interference. Besides sound waves, we are surrounded by another form of waves more difficult to sense. We are constantly exposed to all frequencies and intensities of nonionizing radiation. Most of this radiation passes right through us and is barely perceptible. Infrared radiation, which we experience as heat, does have the ability to significantly increase tissue temperatures. Microwave radiation at certain intensities has the ability to heat tissue by oscillating molecules such as water, thus creating friction and heat. Most radio waves and ELF waves pass right through us with little to no effect. The radio waves from your favorite FM radio station easily pass through your house or your car and most certainly pass through you undetected.

Dr. Brett Says

- Once we become aware of the invisible soup of waves in which we exist, we start to realize that it is quite likely that invisible fields have a greater effect on us than we realize. At any given moment, we are penetrated by waves from radio stations, satellite television transmissions, cellular telephone signals, wireless router signals, baby monitors, radio waves and microwaves from the sun, and much more. Let's not forget that many animals navigate by following invisible magnetic field lines from the earth. You, too, have crystals of magnetite in your brain which are affected by the earth's magnetic field, although we have lost the ability to detect the minute rotations of the magnetite in the pineal gland. Did you know that there are more heart attacks and spikes in blood pressure when the sun is highly active during a solar storm? We clearly need to recognize the effect that these invisible electromagnetic fields have on us.

The explosion in the use of communication technologies that employ low-intensity microwave frequencies, such as cellular phones, cordless phones, wireless routers, and baby monitors, has created a foreign environment of frequencies that, while they do not likely cause significant damage, may have more subtle, long-term, cumulative effects. All these man-made frequencies must regularly interfere with other waves of similar frequencies and create spikes in amplitudes (constructive interference) that may cause tissue heating or cellular damage. This is the uncontrollable aspect of adding an infinite number of similar frequencies to our environment. I will discuss more about this soup of man-made electromagnetic waves called *electrosmog* in chapter 7.

Another source of natural, nonionizing radiation are *Schumann resonances*. Schumann resonances are the natural background electromagnetic radiation of ELF waves caused by the continuous electrical discharges of lightning strikes all over the planet. These regular lightning strikes create background frequencies ranging from 3 Hz to 60 Hz (figure 10). Winifred Otto Schumann first predicted their existence mathematically in 1952. The over two thousand lightning strikes at any given moment on the planet give rise to approximately fifty global lightning strikes per second. The average or base frequency around our planet is approximately 7.83 Hz. The other frequency spikes, which occur at regular intervals over twenty-four hours, are approximately 14.1 Hz, 20.3 Hz, 26.4 Hz, and 32.4 Hz (figure 11).

Figure 10. Schumann Resonances
By Andrzej Brodziak (Own work) [Public domain], via Wikimedia Commons

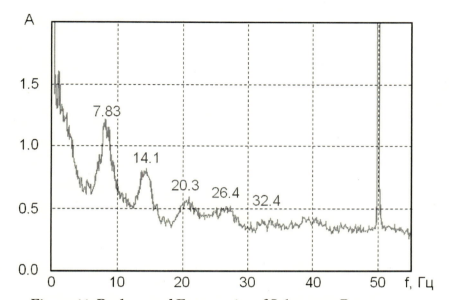

Figure 11. Background Frequencies of Schumann Resonances
By AdmiralHood (Own work) [CC-BY-SA-3.0 (http://creativecommons.org/licenses/by-sa/3.0) or GFDL (http://www.gnu.org/copyleft/fdl.html)], via Wikimedia Commons

It is interesting to note that these background frequencies are similar to the brain wave frequencies shown in figure 6. Recall that theta waves (associated with sleep and deep relaxation) are 4 to 7 Hz. Alpha waves (associated with relaxation and calm) are 8 to 13 Hz. Beta waves (associated with active thinking and problem-solving) are 13 to 38 Hz, and Gamma waves (associated with complex and coordinated brain activities) are 30 to 100 Hz.

What does this mean? Some have suggested that we might be hardwired to be in tune with the earth's natural background Schumann resonances. Research has demonstrated that Schumann resonances increase in frequency in the morning and start to decrease in the evening. Perhaps we are more in tune with earth than we thought. Perhaps the Schumann resonances help us to establish our own natural rhythms

Dr. Brett Says

- Schumann resonances are another indication that we have evolved to be responsive to these invisible electromagnetic fields. It is important to note that the magnetic field strength of the Schumann resonances is thousands of times weaker than the magnetic fields of many of our household appliances and wirings. Being surrounded by electromagnetic fields is not so much of a concern; rather, the ever-increasing amount of power used by man-made sources to operate all these appliances might be of concern. Even more worrying is the unintended constructive interference resulting when numerous waves of similar frequencies meet.

In Summary

- Humans produce and respond to a wide range of both ionizing and nonionizing wave frequencies.
- The nonionizing radiation produced by humans is created by: ion movement, reflection of visible light, production of ultraviolet biophotons, and production of infrared light.
- In constructive interference, waves of similar frequencies interact and summate; therefore, you literally feel more energy from things or people with similar base frequencies. They are *wave amplifiers*.
- Conversely, things or people with opposite base frequencies can be *wave reducers*.
- One base frequency is not better or more desirable than another. The Ekahi Method teaches you to honor your base frequency and nourish it.
- We have evolved to be responsive to our natural, environmental soup of electromagnetic frequencies, but the man-made sources are using much more power than we have adapted to.

The Ekahi Method

PART I
Discover Your Base Frequency

CHAPTER 4

Finding Your Base Frequency

And you? When will you begin that long journey into yourself?
—*Rumi*

As I mentioned in the preface of this book, the Ekahi Method uses science as its backbone. In this chapter you will learn to measure your own frequency. You will become skilled at measuring the electrical activity in the body through simple and practical means. Once you master this skill in yourself, the Ekahi Method will show you how to measure this frequency in other people—from a distance. The great power of the Ekahi Method is that it teaches awareness of other people's frequencies and how to adjust our own frequencies to respond to different situations, such as resolving conflict or improving communication.

Before we go any further, you need to complete the *frequency profile*. The frequency profile is an objective assessment of your *base frequency*. I have used this profile with patients for many years. As mentioned, the unique aspect of the frequency profile is that it objectifies frequency. Many other tests indirectly assess your natural energy by asking questions about your personality or interests and by taking into account your physical characteristics. While these types of tests can provide some valuable information, they do not address the person's natural base frequency.

The first two sections of the frequency profile require you to measure both your *resting heart rate* and your *resting respiratory rate* (breathing rate)—this is not difficult. The remaining seven questions relate to your frequency. There are questions about your sleep and digestive cycles, preferred type of activity and climate, how you learn best, and adjectives that describe you. These seven questions are loosely based on *Ayurveda*, the most ancient form of medicine known. Its earliest writings are in the *Vedas*, ancient Hindu texts written in Sanskrit approximately between 1000 and 1500 BC.

In Ayurveda, a physician examines a patient much like a Western doctor does today. The Ayurvedic physician would examine your pulse, your skin, your tongue, your hair, your breath, and your waste products, and ask numerous questions about your overall state of health. The physician would then classify the patient into one of three main categories, or *doshas*: *kapha*, *pitta*, or *vata*. People of a specific dosha had a predictable body type and physiology. When a person was unwell, the illness was predictable in terms of the location and general symptoms for each of the doshas.

While some of the questions asked in an Ayurvedic dosha exam pertain to frequency, many questions relate to anatomy and aspects of physiology unique to Ayurveda. Some of the questions in the *frequency profile* were adapted from Ayurveda. I have statistically analyzed each of the questions for its validity. This is one of the key features of the Ekahi Method's frequency profile: it blends some aspects of ancient wisdom with modern science. The frequency profile is unique because it uses objective measures such as resting heart rate and resting respiratory rate, in addition to some questions related to natural frequency.

Once you develop the ability to sense and appreciate your own frequency, you will learn how to indirectly measure somebody else's frequency. Understanding your own frequency and being able to sense those of other people are the skills required to effectively use the Ekahi Method.

How to Complete the Frequency Profile

You will be measuring two important physiological aspects of yourself: heart rate and breathing rate. Make sure to take your heart rate and breathing rate when you wake up in the morning and before you get out of bed for the greatest accuracy.

You will then answer seven additional questions which relate to your natural energy. As you answer the questions, *think of yourself in a period of stability*, not necessarily how you feel right at that moment. If you are having difficulty answering any of the questions, it is a good idea to also ask someone who knows you very well for their opinion. Ask them how they would answer the question for you. Sometimes others perceive us better than we perceive ourselves.

Some Important Things to Note about Using This Profile

- The frequency profile takes approximately fifteen minutes to complete. Plan to set aside this amount of time one morning and perform the first two objective measurements (heart rate and respiratory rate) while lying in bed. Put a stopwatch beside your bed the night before.
- Questions 3 to 9 assess your qualities when you are mentally and physically stable. The questions are not necessarily about how you feel right now, but about how you would describe yourself most of the time.
- If you are having trouble answering a question, ask somebody who knows you well and has known you for most of your life.

- The measurements must be taken during a state of relative health.
- Do not take the measurements while affected by stimulants or depressants such as caffeine or alcohol.
- The test is most accurate for adults between 18 and 75 who are free of significant diseases and not taking medications which may alter heart rate.

Important Point

- No one base frequency (color) is better or worse than another.
- Your base frequency is not a reflection of your health or fitness, nor is it a judgment of your character.
- Your base frequency is a reflection of your natural rate of energy production.
- Do not select a category because you think it has better characteristics.
- All base frequency colors are wonderful!

Measuring Your Resting Heart Rate and Resting Respiratory Rate

Place a watch or clock with seconds displayed beside your bed the night before you plan to measure your resting heart rate and resting respiratory rate.

In the morning after you wake, while you are still lying in bed, find your pulse by feeling either your radial pulse on your wrist (figure 12) or your carotid pulse on the side of your neck (figure 13). Lightly press with your index and middle finger until you can feel the pulse. Look at your watch/clock. Count the number of beats over sixty seconds. Record this number in the Resting Heart Rate section of the frequency profile (table 3) and check the column that fits your range.

Figure 12. Taking a Radial Pulse

Figure 13. Taking a Carotid Pulse.

Next, place your hand on your chest. Look at your watch/clock and count the rises of your chest over sixty seconds. Record this number in the Resting Respiratory Rate section of the Frequency Profile (table 3) and check the column that fits your range.

Now complete the remaining sections of the profile. In each row, do not check any more than *one* box.

Table 3. The Ekahi Method: *Frequency Profile*

	Red	Yellow	Green	Blue	Violet
Resting Heart Rate: ____ (beats per minute)	☐ Less than 62	☐ 62-66	☐ 67-71	☐ 72-76	☐ Greater than 76
Resting Respiratory Rate: ____ (respirations per minute)	☐ Less than 9	☐ 10-12	☐ 13-15	☐ 16-18	☐ Greater than 18
Sleep Cycle	☐ Sleep soundly, naturally wake up after nine in the morning. Preference for staying up late and sleeping late.	☐ Sleep soundly, naturally wake up between eight and nine. Preference for staying up later in the evening.	☐ Moderately sound sleep, naturally wake up between seven and eight. Preference to go to bed midevening.	☐ Light sleeper, naturally wake up between six and seven. Early to bed and early to rise.	☐ Restless sleeper (toss and turn), naturally wake up before six. Early to bed.
Daily Energy	☐ Slow to start in the morning, but good endurance throughout day and into late evening.	☐ Moderate energy in the morning, but more energy as the day progresses. Most energy later in the day.	☐ From morning to early evening, have a steady amount of energy.	☐ Fairly high energy throughout the day, with a couple of bouts of fatigue. Tired in evening.	☐ Tend to have bursts of energy throughout day and tire easily.
Words That Describe You	☐ Calm Observant	☐ Adaptable Reflective	☐ Focused Competitive	☐ Excitable Driven	☐ Talkative Reactive

The Ekahi Method

	Red	Yellow	Green	Blue	Violet
How You Process New Information	☐ Independent learner. Intuitive and reflective. Process slowly but with excellent retention.	☐ Independent learner. Experiential learner. Methodically process with good retention.	☐ Logical and detail oriented. Analytical. Process quickly and with good retention.	☐ Enjoy some group learning but prefer to lead. Learn best when able to move. Learn quickly but selective retention.	☐ Learn best with others or in group. Like to discuss the process of learning. Learn quickly but prone to forget quickly.
Your Metabolism	☐ Can go for long periods (more than four hours) between meals. No food or digestive sensitivities.	☐ Eat three meals a day and generally don't need snacks. No food or digestive sensitivities.	☐ Must eat three meals daily at regular three- to four-hour intervals, and need snacks. Few food or digestive sensitivities.	☐ Regular meal or snack needed every two to three hours. Some food and digestive sensitivities.	☐ Must eat small meal or snack every one to two hours. Problems with digestion and prone to food sensitivities.
Activity and Exercise Preference	☐ Noncompetitive exercise that is low in intensity but lasts for longer periods.	☐ Enjoy a balance of low intensity activity and occasional competive sports.	☐ Prefer competitive sports or activities with a purpose.	☐ Prefer social and group activities (running groups, spin classes). Like to see results and compare with others.	☐ Prefer activities that are social and involve body movement (yoga, dance, tai chi).
Environmental Preference	☐ Adaptable to most temperatures but dislike cold, damp, and humid environments.	☐ Adaptable to most temperatures with a preference for drier environments.	☐ Dislike too much heat. Usually feel warm.	☐ Prefer warm temperatures and some humidity. Tendency to feel cold and dry.	☐ Require heat and humidity. Frequently feel cold and dry. Hands and feet often cold.
Column Totals:	Red: _____	Yellow: _____	Green: _____	Blue: _____	Violet: _____

Brett Wade, PhD

Scoring the Frequency Profile

Total the number of checks in each of the five columns to determine your frequency color. *The column with the most marks is your base frequency color.* You are either red, yellow, green, blue, or violet.

It is very common to have a few answers in each section. This may indicate an inaccurate measurement of resting heart rate and resting respiratory rate or that you did not answering questions from the perspective of a period of stability in your life. If you have a wide spread of scores over multiple columns, it is a good idea to leave the profile for a day. Then try another reading of resting heart rate and resting respiratory rate, and have somebody who knows you well help to answer any of the sections you are uncertain about.

What if two or more of your highest columns are a tie?

This is also very common. Look at the column where your respiratory rate is; that is your base frequency. Our research and data, collected over years of developing the frequency profile, show that respiratory rate is the most statistically valid indicator or base frequency.

My base frequency is: _____

Remember: All base frequencies are wonderful. No one color is better than another and no color is more or less desirable than another. Your base frequency has nothing to do with your favorite color. Once you know your base frequency, you can learn to respect and honor your natural waves and to temporarily adjust (*frequency tune*) your waves for success. This is part of learning to master the waves of life.

In table 4 are some general descriptions of the energies of each base frequency as they relate to physical qualities, emotional and mental qualities, social qualities, sleep, digestion, and metabolism. These are descriptions for typical examples of each base frequency; not every descriptor will match your personal feelings or energies. In subsequent chapters, we will flesh out the personal aspects of your base frequency, such as your wave amplifiers, wave reducers, and natural zone, which make you unique.

Table 4. Typical Energy Descriptions for Each Base Frequency

	Physical	Emotional and Mental	Social	Sleep	Eating and Digestion
Red	Reds are slow to start the day. They tend to have a guarded posture with closed body language. They move slowly and speak in a calm and relaxed tone. Reds enjoy activities that take advantage of their excellent endurance.	Reds do not anger easily and are generally calm, observant, thoughtful, and sensitive. Often described as easygoing and compassionate.	Reds are generally hard to get to know. They prefer conversing with smaller numbers of people and to listen rather than speak. They are naturally good listeners.	Reds generally sleep soundly for at least eight hours a night. Often reds prefer to stay up late and sleep late.	They tend to have good digestive systems and very rarely have food sensitivities. They can go for long periods without experiencing hunger.
Yellow	They generally have steady energy that builds through the day. They generally have closed body language but will move toward being more open as needed. Yellows speak in calm and relaxed tones. Yellows like to regularly push the limits of their naturally good stamina and strength.	Yellows are fairly easygoing by nature but have the ability to rapidly increase their amplitude (intensity) to accomplish tasks and goals. This makes yellow quite adaptable.	They prefer speaking in smaller groups. They may be more prone to cross their arms in conversation but they are good listeners.	Yellows tend to sleep soundly and generally sleep undisturbed for seven to eight hours. Similar to reds, they have a preference for staying up later.	Yellows generally have very few digestive problems. They can go three to four hours between meals without feeling hungry.
Green	From the time they wake up until they go to bed, greens have steady energy. They tend to possess an athletic build and tone with a forward-leaning body language. They like to be active with a purpose. Greens enjoy sports or activities that take advantage of their excellent strength and competitive nature.	Greens can be aggressive and competitive and they enjoy challenges. They tend to have sharp minds and excellent ability to concentrate. They can anger easily.	Greens enjoy leading a group. They enjoy vigorous debate and discussion. They have penetrating eye contact and dominant body language.	Greens are moderately deep sleepers. They tend to wake up naturally before seven in the morning. They regularly prefer to sleep eight to nine hours.	Greens eat regularly every three to four hours. Their naturally strong digestions and metabolisms cause them to have a higher body temperature; they may perspire more than other frequencies.

Blue	The energy of blues typically has at least one or two dips during the day and quickly tails off in the early evening. They tend to have upright and erect posture and active body language with a high rate of speech. Blues prefer activities that are social and mildly competitive.	Blues have active and creative minds and like change. They are generally outgoing and gregarious. Often described as driven and self-assured. They can anger easily but it often passes quickly.	They are enthusiastic in conversation and enjoy being around lots of people. They like to lead groups and are hand-talkers with lots of head and body movement.	Blues are light sleepers and often wake up a couple of times a night. They wake naturally between six and seven in the morning.	Blues need to eat every couple of hours. They may suffer from some minor digestive sensitivities.
Violet	Violets go through their day with short bursts of energy and tire easily. They tend to move, act, and speak quickly; they almost appear to vibrate. They have open body language. Violets prefer activities that involve rhythmic movements and have a social component.	Violets have an excitable and fun-loving personality. They often report feeling anxious and they may be easily distracted.	They like to be surrounded by people for short periods of time. They appear to be very social and are usually quite talkative. Since violets' energy dips several times a day, they need to frequently recharge.	Violets do not sleep soundly. They toss and turn and wake up naturally before six in the morning. They go to bed relatively early in the evening.	Violets must eat every couple of hours. They regularly eat small meals and are the most prone of all the base frequencies to digestive problems.

CHAPTER 5

Understanding Your Base Frequency

Knowing yourself is the beginning of all wisdom.
—Aristotle

Now that you know your *base frequency*, what does it tell you? It has nothing to do with your favorite color or which color looks best on you. The classification of your color relates to the frequency of the spectrum of colors in the rainbow—red, orange, yellow, green, blue, indigo, violet—red having the lowest frequency and violet the highest. The *frequency profile* assigned you to a *base frequency*. While base frequency alone does not tell you the specifics of one's personality, likes/dislikes, interests, or hobbies, it does elucidate one's natural rhythms and energy. Remember that *frequency* is the number of times a waves rises and falls in a period of time. The closer your base frequency is to violet, the higher your frequency; the closer your base frequency is to red, the lower your frequency.

Important Point

- Remember: Whether your frequency is high (violet) or low (red) has nothing to do with intelligence or looks or success.

This measure merely helps you understand the rate at which your body produces and emits energy.

In compiling data from the frequency profile over many years, I have noticed that people seem to enjoy the company of those with the same base frequency than that of others. Why is this? Recall that if two waves of similar frequencies meet, they summate and increase intensity (constructive interference). This increased intensity is often felt as a rise in energy. Therefore, people of the same frequency class tend to energize each other; they are *wave amplifiers*. Conversely, people of opposite frequency classes tend to cancel out each other's frequency and drain each other's energy; they are *wave reducers*. Most of the time, however, other people have more subtle effects on our energy, either raising or lowering it only slightly. Often the effect is so subtle that we are unaware of it. The Ekahi Method will now make you much more conscious of your wave reducers and wave amplifiers.

Dr. Brett Says

- Your base frequency is like your fingerprint. While the Ekahi Method categorizes base frequency into five colors, nobody else—not even those who share the same color as you—has a frequency that responds to the same wave reducers and wave amplifiers as yours does. Nobody has waves that rise and fall to the same heights as your wave does. It is important that you start to get in touch with your base frequency and your wave reducers and wave amplifiers so that you can learn to *master the waves of life*.

An Exercise

Since we are starting the process of getting in touch with your base frequency, let's begin by answering some questions that will help you really get to know your waves.

Describe your energy throughout a typical day. When does your peak(s) of energy occur?
Example: My peak energies are at ten in the morning, two in the afternoon, and six in the evening.
_____
_____

Who are your wave reducers? (people who seem to drain your energy)
Example: Bob at work, the security guy at front door, the barista at the coffee shop, my brother.
_____
_____

What else is a wave reducer for you? (foods, drinks, music, temperatures, places, etc.)
Example: Heavy foods with dairy, alcohol, classical music, cold and damp weather, Las Vegas.
_____
_____

Who are your wave amplifiers? (people who raise your energy)
Example: My partner, my cousin, Sally at work, my best friend John.
_____
_____

What else is a wave amplifier for you? (foods, drinks, music, temperatures, places, etc.)
Example: Chicken salad, dark chocolate, coffee, jazz music, warm and dry weather, Sedona, Arizona.
_____
_____

Brett Wade, PhD

What To Do With This Information

These are the first steps to understanding your base frequency. In later chapters we will learn what it feels like when your base frequency is out of balance and needs to be reset. By identifying our wave reducers and wave amplifiers, we can start to find the *natural zone* of our waves. Part 5 of the Ekahi Method teaches you how to surround yourself with resonant frequencies to maintain your physical and emotional health and settle into your natural zone. You can right now start by being aware of the power of your wave amplifiers and wave reducers. Start respecting and honoring your base frequency.

Case Study

> Chronic fatigue syndrome (CFS) is a debilitating disorder of extreme fatigue that is not improved by sleep. Its onset may sometimes be related to a virus or a stressful life event. The patient's immune system overreacts and starts producing more white blood cells, sending a signal to the body that an invader has entered and must be dealt with. Most people experience this as flu-like symptoms. In addition to feeling fatigue, people with CFS often feel like they always have the flu.
>
> A patient of mine suffered symptoms related to CFS for years. She was twenty-five when I first evaluated her. She reported that extreme fatigue and flu-like symptoms began shortly after her mother unexpectedly passed away. When I saw her in my office, she had the pale look of somebody who was gravely ill. She was cold, dressed in a warm sweater in July. She spoke softly and stared at the ground with her shoulders hunched.

She told me that prior to her mom passing away about a year ago, she had had a job as a manager of a retail store. She had exercised five days a week, maintained a healthy diet, and had a rich social life. She had also been engaged to be married. One year after her mother's death, this woman was unemployed and reclusive—she barely saw her friends. She did not exercise, ate mainly fast food, and had gained twenty pounds. Her fiancé had called the engagement off.

After taking down my patient's history and performing a physical assessment, it was clear that there was nothing physically wrong with her body. She was clearly debilitated and, without question, her energy was low. I needed to learn more about my patient's lifestyle. It turned out that after her mom died, she had moved out of her own apartment to live with her dad in order to support him. I asked how she felt about living with her dad. She made a movement to readjust her posture and replied, "Fine. He is a good man, and he just needs my help right now."

Something about her unconscious adjustment of body language made me think that, although her dad seemed like a good person and she truly loved him, something was affecting her on an unconscious level. I asked my patient if she would complete a frequency profile and have her dad complete one as well. She agreed and when she returned a week later, I examined the results. It was no surprise that she and her father were opposite frequencies. He was a red base frequency and she was a violet. While I have met people in successful long-term relationships who are opposites on the frequency profile, it can be de-energizing for them.

I suggested to my patient that she follow the Ekahi Method to nourish her body with resonant frequencies, including food and exercise suitable to her frequency profile. I also suggested she spend as much time in nature as possible and find one person with whom she felt comfortable socializing at least once a week. I needed her to consider the fact that her and her father's opposite frequencies were draining her energy. I explained the importance of finding the natural zone for her energy.

One month later, my patient returned. I could tell she was better, even from a distance. Her posture had improved, her skin tone was better, and she seemed more confident. She reported that she felt much better and had started to lightly exercise again. She was optimistic, as was I, about making an even greater recovery. She still lives with her dad but now balances her life by spending time with people of resonant frequencies and by nourishing her body with food and exercise suitable for her violet base frequency.

If you are thinking to yourself that this is an extreme case study, I can tell you that many of my patients with chronic diseases have stories similar to this one. I believe that to achieve optimal health, one needs to understand one's own base frequency and the effect that the external environment has on it. It is vital that people learn how to regularly reset their rhythms and nourish their base frequency.

Important Point

- It is vital to know your *base frequency* so that you know what it feels like when you are out of balance.
- It is helpful to know other people's base frequencies so you can understand how your waves interact with each other (how to raise or lower the amplitude or energy).

- Numerous uncontrolled *wave reducers* and w*ave amplifiers* can actually move you to a different base frequency!
- We are intermittently forced to an unnatural base frequency. If we do not reset, this could lead to living life in an unnatural base frequency.

Finding the Natural Zone on Your Wave

You now know your base frequency. The *natural zone* in the Ekahi Method is the natural cycling of the amplitude of your waves, when the waves are not too high and not too low. The graph below shows an example of a base frequency with a couple of peaks of energy in the day and a lull around midday. On the left-hand side of the graph, there is an arbitrary scale of 0 to 5, with 5 being maximum energy. The bottom of the graph is a twenty-four-hour clock. The two peaks are at approximately 8:00 a.m. and 18:00 (6:00 p.m.). Notice how the energy stays somewhat in the middle of the energy ranges. This is the natural zone. The words on the left-hand side of the graph describe emotions and feelings often associated with the natural zone.

- control
- balance
- ease
- comfort
- happiness
- fluidity
- effortlessness
- power
- lightness

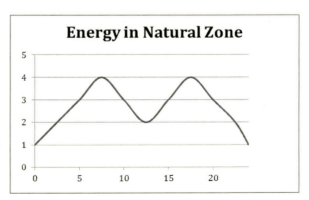

Figure 14. Energy in the Natural Zone

Important Point

- You might think that you can keep your base frequency always in the *natural zone*, but that is not realistic. Numerous uncontrollable factors will push your waves higher or lower. You can't control all the external factors of life; it is important to realize that the ride up and down is very normal. What is not normal is riding too high for too long, or riding too low for too long. We will learn in part 3 of the Ekahi Method that being in balance is being in the natural zone of your own base frequency.

Energy Riding Too Low in Your Base Frequency

Let's now take a look at a base frequency wave that is too low or too shallow. There are still two peaks of energy—this is typical for this base frequency—but notice that the energy never climbs above 2. Emotions or feelings associated with energy riding low are listed on the left-hand side of the graph.

- fatigue
- logyness
- depression
- pessimism
- heaviness
- slow movements
- foggy brain
- difficulty concentrating
- forgetfulness
- apathy

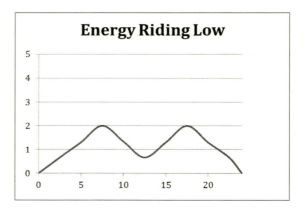

Figure 15. Energy Riding Too Low

Energy Riding Too High in Your Base Frequency

You can also start to feel unnatural if you have been riding high too high on your base frequency for too long. In this graph, there are still two peaks of energy, but the energy never drops below 3. Emotions or feelings associated with energy riding too high are listed on the left-hand side of the graph.

- anxious
- nervous
- paranoid
- jittery
- aggressive
- over reactive
- snappish
- frazzled
- short-fused
- burned out

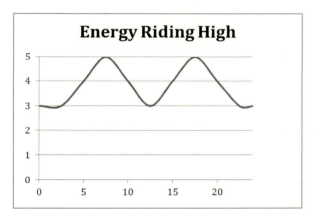

Figure 16. Energy Riding Too High

Special Category: The Big Wave Riders

Within each base frequency, there is a small percentage whom I call the *big wave riders*. Before you start thinking that this sounds like a good category to be in, let me remind you that the only amplitude-adjusting you want to do is to find the natural zone in your base frequency. Big wave riders never decided to be that way; they were born that way. When in balance, the natural zone of a big wave rider is represented by massive fluctuations in energy. Big wave riders regularly exhaust their energy and may, in fact, bottom out for several days before coming back up again.

In this graph, notice that the energy swings from rock bottom straight back up to the top. These extreme fluctuations could be spread over several days, but the person will eventually ride both extremes of the wave. Emotions or feelings associated with big wave riding are listed on the left-hand side of the graph.

- euphoria
- mania
- overconfidence
- powerfulness
- fear
- depression
- anxiety
- paranoia

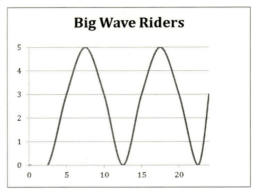

Figure 17. Energy of Big Wave Riders

In the next chapter we will learn how external environments such as other people can affect our energy by acting as wave reducers, causing us to ride too low. Wave reducers may be people or unnatural environments such as electrosmog (chapter 7).

Important Point

- Too many external uncontrolled wave amplifiers and wave reducers can actually move you out of your base frequency.
- Imagine moving your hand up and down in a bucket of water at your natural frequency. The waves you create are lapping up the sides of the bucket. Now imagine somebody else puts their hand into the bucket and moves it up and down at their frequency, which is very different from yours. The result is a new wave that is a messy combination of both

original waves (interference). You have been pulled out of your base frequency.

In subsequent chapters you will learn to *reset to your base frequency* and to *nourish your base frequency*. These techniques will help you find the natural zone on your wave. You must also be very cognizant of the effects of your wave reducers and wave amplifiers. While you can learn to effectively use your own wave amplifiers and wave reducers, uncontrolled external ones may knock you out of your base frequency if you are regularly exposed to them.

An Exercise

In the previous exercise, I asked you to record your natural energy cycle during the day and some of your wave reducers and wave amplifiers. Now you know the times of day when you naturally come down from the peak of your wave and the times of day when you naturally come to the top of your wave.

Many people abuse substances like caffeine, alcohol, nicotine, sweet or fatty foods, and prescription drugs to alter their positions on the wave. For those with certain medical conditions, this is necessary due to the extremes of their highs and/or lows. But the majority of people need to find less abusive and addictive means to return to the natural zone. *Personal wave reducers* are the things you can do to effectively and safely come down off your wave. *Personal wave amplifiers* are the things you can do to effectively and safely raise your wave. Now I would like you to think about what you can do when you feel you have been riding too low for too long, or too high for too long.

Five things I can do to help me find my natural zone if I have been riding too low for too long (personal wave amplifiers):
Examples: Talk to a friend, light aerobic exercise, go out for dinner, journal my feelings, try something new like an art class or dance class, explore a new

hobby, do some aromatherapy, go to a garden center, go to an art gallery, watch a good movie.

_____
_____
_____
_____

Five things I can do to help me find my natural zone if I have been riding too high for too long (personal wave reducers):
Examples: Try a calming tea, take a warm bath, talk to a friend, take a long walk, meditate, lie on the floor with somebody I love, journal my feelings, eat a carbohydrate meal with some protein, light a candle with a calming scent, have a massage, wrap myself in a warm blanket.

_____
_____
_____
_____

Dr. Brett Says

- You might be asking yourself how wave amplifiers, wave reducers, and the natural zone relate to your base frequency. Your base frequency is the rate at which you make waves. Violets produce waves more rapidly than reds do. The nature of waves is that they move up and down. When your waves are high, you feel energetic and maybe even a bit anxious. When your waves are low, you feel tired and maybe a bit depressed. Somewhere in the middle is your natural zone. We all naturally move through our waves, going up and down with the accompanying emotions. If we are feeling too high on our wave or too low, we can use our own personal wave amplifiers and personal wave reducers to bring us toward our natural zone. Uncontrolled wave amplifiers and reducers can actually move us out of our base frequency. Being out of base frequency too long can lead to disease. People of base frequencies opposite to ours, certain sounds and lighting, and electrosmog can actually push our waves around so much that we adopt an unnatural frequency!

There are four things that can force you out of your base frequency: (1) subconsciously adopting somebody else's base frequency, (2) purposely adjusting your base frequency to suit an environment or person, (3) exposure to unrelenting and uncontrolled wave reducers and wave amplifiers, and (4) exposure to an unrelenting environment of discordant frequencies (for example, electrosmog).

In Summary

- Your base frequency is your natural frequency. What makes you unique is your own natural zone within your base frequency.
- For each base frequency, there are general traits common to everyone of that color.
- You now know what your daily energy looks like and some of your external uncontrolled wave reducers and wave amplifiers.
- Regular exposure to these uncontrolled wave reducers and amplifiers can knock you out of base frequency.
- You should identify your personal wave amplifiers and personal wave reducers; they can be used to safely bring you up or down your wave.
- You should have some strategies to help you find your natural zone.
- Know that you will naturally ride from the top to the bottom of your wave. The danger is staying at either extreme for too long.

PART II
Sense External Frequencies

CHAPTER 6

Sensing Frequencies in Other People

We are all connected;
To each other, biologically. To the earth, chemically.
To the rest of the universe, atomically.
—Neil deGrasse Tyson

We now know how to assess our own *base frequency* and we are starting to understand the concept of finding the *natural zone* of our wave. In the previous case study, I showed you how spending too much time with people of opposite base frequencies can be draining and even negatively affect your health. The best way to measure the frequency of another person would be to give them the frequency profile—of course, this is not always practical.

It is not a bad idea to determine whether you and your partner have similar frequency classes. Remember that even if you have a very different frequency from your partner, it is still possible to have a successful long-term relationship. In fact, I have met many couples who intuitively worked out how to have a happy and healthy life together by nourishing their respective frequencies and not spending all of their time together only. In other words, having friends of similar frequencies is crucial.

With the exception of our friends and our partners, most of the people we interact with in our lives (coworkers, neighbors, family) are not people we choose to spend our time with. Yet most of our day is spent in environments with these people of other frequencies; we have to figure out how to make it work.

So how do you know when you are in sync with somebody such as a coworker or a neighbor? For the most part, it is pretty easy to tell; you just seem to enjoy their company. If you pay attention to people who are in sync and engaged in conversation, you will see that they exhibit almost matched physical positions and actions such as posture, the way the hold their arms, hand-talking, head-nodding, and making comments or sounds during listening. These people will likely speak at the same rate and have similar body language.

The old saying, "Like likes like," is often true. Either consciously or subconsciously, we tend to enjoy the company of people who are similar to us in frequency. This does not mean that people of similar frequencies will definitely have the same personality type or the same interests. To discover whether somebody has a similar frequency to you, you must sense more subtle signs. You can observe body language and body movement, and you can detect the effect of different energies on your own physiology. Remember that somebody who has a similar energy to you will raise your energy, and that an opposite energy will drain you. Develop your skills to see if you can start sensing people's frequency from several feet away.

By remote-sensing this way, you have a better chance of determining a person's base frequency. If you engage in conversation, it is possible that the person will have the natural ability to match your frequency—some people have this natural gift—and what we are trying to determine is the person's base frequency, not their adjusted frequency. (I will teach you the vital skill of frequency matching in later chapters.)

So let's begin by observing people. See if you can start to imagine which frequency class they may fit into. Here are some things you can observe for each of the frequency classes.

Observations of Red Frequency Class

- Reds tend to move slowly and speak in a calm and relaxed tone.
- They will generally exhibit closed body language (arms crossed or kept close to body).
- They may appear shy.
- Eye contact will be limited unless they are engaged in meaningful conversation.
- They are cautious when meeting new people as they feel too much.
- They are relatively hard to get to know.
- They prefer conversation with smaller numbers of people and to listen rather than speak.
- They are naturally good listeners and are often described as easygoing and compassionate.
- They will exit social situations quietly without drawing attention.
- They do not anger easily.
- They have excellent ability to focus on a singular task by themselves.

Observations of Yellow Frequency Class

- Yellows are similar to reds in that they speak in calm and relaxed tones and prefer speaking in smaller groups.

- Their body language is slightly more active than that of reds. They may be more prone to cross their arms in conversation, but they are good listeners.
- They fluctuate between appearing extremely interested in conversation and detached from it.
- They are selective with eye contact and use it as needed.
- Yellows are also easygoing by nature but have the ability to rapidly increase their amplitude to accomplish tasks and goals.
- They are naturally hard on themselves and take responsibility for their own actions.
- They are better suited to leading a group than reds but not as dominant in this regard as greens.
- Yellows people prefer to think before acting and speaking.

Observations of Green Frequency Class

- Greens tend to possess an athletic build and tone.
- They tend to have a sharp mind and excellent ability to concentrate.
- They can be aggressive and competitive and enjoy challenges.
- In conversation, they maintain eye contact and have a focused, penetrating look.
- They engage fully in conversation with a balance of listening and speaking. They tend to lean forward and generally like to dominate the conversation.
- They enjoy debate and rhetoric.
- They are born leaders.
- Their naturally strong digestive system and metabolism cause them to have a higher body temperature; they may perspire more than other frequencies.

Observations of Blue Frequency Class

- Blues tend to have upright and erect posture and active body language.
- They are enthusiastic in conversation and enjoy being around lots of people. They are not self-conscious in conversation, which frees them to speak easily with just about everybody.
- They like to lead groups and are obvious hand-talkers with lots of head and body movement.
- They maintain eye contact and tend to have intensity in their eyes when speaking.
- They may speak about topics with intensity and passion.
- They have active and creative minds and like change.
- They are generally outgoing and gregarious and have a naturally quick rate of speech.

Observations of Violet Frequency Class

- Violets tend to move, act, speak, and think quickly.
- They almost appear to vibrate when you observe them.
- They have an excitable and fun-loving personality.
- They appear to make friends quickly.
- They make eye contact for brief but intense periods, quickly moving focus between everybody in the vicinity.
- They are quick to learn new things but quickly forget what they have learned.
- They go through their day with short bursts of energy and tire easily.
- They like to be surrounded by people for short period of time.
- They have open body language and an undefined sense of personal space; they may get close and use touch frequently.

An Exercise

Practice trying to identify the frequency classes of strangers in a public setting. I regularly do this at restaurants, at the park, or at the beach. I have developed the ability to sense by observation those who will likely have the same frequency as me. I confirm this by walking near them and seeing if my energy is affected. I may notice a slight increase in my heart rate or my breathing rate.

Find a public place, such as a mall or a park, that has lots of people but is not so crowded you can't separate one person's energy from the next. Using the above descriptions for each frequency class, see if you can observe these characteristics in people. Let's start by trying to find people in our own base frequency class.

These are some of the things you should be looking for:

- How fast does he/she speak?
- How fast does he/she walk?
- Is his/her posture relaxed or tense?
- Is his/her body language open or closed?
- What is his/her sense of personal space? Does he/she appear to be in close contact with others in conversation?
- Is he/she a hand-talkers? Does he/she have active body language in conversation?
- Does he/she seem unable to focus in conversation?
- Is he/she fidgeting or relaxed? Sitting or standing?
- Is his/her eye contact focused or relaxed?
- Is his/her eye contact intense or minimal?
- Is his/her breathing rate rapid and shallow, or deep and slow?
- Does he/she appear to be dressed too warmly or too coolly?

Once you have identified a person you think has a similar frequency to you, walk by them and see if you notice a change in your own amplitude or frequency. Do not speak to this person or linger in their vicinity, but walk by them at your normal pace, keeping a natural distance as if you were passing each other on the sidewalk.

If the person is indeed the same frequency as you, you might notice

- a slight increase in feelings of excitement,
- a possible slight increase in heart rate,
- a possible slight increase in respiratory rate, or
- an almost magnetic attraction that is not at all based on appearance.

Continue to practice this skill at a safe distance until you are able to detect changes in your physiology. Once you can notice increases in energy with people whom you have identified as having the same frequency as you, repeat the experiment with people who appear to have very different frequencies from yours. Continue to maintain a safe distance and do not make eye contact with or speak to the person.

When you encounter somebody with a significantly different frequency from yours, you might notice

- a sense of not wanting to remain in their space for too long;
- a feeling of increased anxiety or stress;
- increased tension in the muscles of your upper shoulders, neck, or jaw;
- an uneasy feeling in your stomach; or
- a feeling that you want to walk away quickly.

After you have spent some time observing other people's frequencies, it is time to evaluate the people in your life closest to you. Begin by observing them with a fresh perspective. Try to guess what their frequency class is and then have them complete the frequency profile.

It is important to understand the frequencies of people around us and even more important to understand the frequencies of those we spend the most time with. In the next section you will learn how you can tune in to other people's frequencies in order to temporarily affect a business relationship, negotiate a purchase, resolve a conflict, or achieve a goal.

How does this work? Remember the principle of constructive interference: when waves of similar frequencies come into contact, they summate and increase the energy of the wave. As we will learn, there are simple ways we can alter, or tune, our own frequency to match the frequency of others to achieve a desired outcome. In fact, many people do this naturally all the time. The problem with spending too much time out of your natural frequency is that it is incredibly fatiguing and can eventually lead to the development of chronic health problems.

Dr. Brett Says

- Some people to lead their lives in a base frequency that is not their own. They are in jobs or relationships in which they feel they have to be like everyone else. But you were born with your own unique base frequency. Trying to live somebody else's base frequency will eventually contribute to disease.

This is why it is so important to understand the base frequency of the people in your life. You are not limited to relationships with people of your base frequency. In my experience, most people in successful relationships have different base frequencies. You must learn to regularly reset to your own base frequency and to find your natural zone in order to live a healthy and happy life. This is part of learning to *master the waves of life*.

What We Actually Detect in Other People

As I mentioned in earlier chapters, humans can emit a wide range of both ionizing and nonionizing wave frequencies. Do you doubt that you have the ability to sense these frequencies? Close your eyes and ask yourself whether you could, from some distance, detect heat from another person? I am certain you could. You would be measuring the infrared radiation coming from that person. In addition to infrared radiation, we emit extremely low frequency radiation, we emit biophotons in the ultraviolet range, we reflect visible light, and we produce audible sound waves.

While some these wave frequencies may be more challenging to sense, once we couple them with some of the typical body language of each base frequency, we can start to develop our ability to intuit somebody's heart rate or breathing rate from a distance. While research into the ability of humans to pick up or sense these biophotons is scant, it makes evolutionary sense that we would be able to detect things as subtle as infrared radiation. Infrared radiation, which is emitted in the form of heat, can be measured easily with infrared thermometers—but might we be able to detect this form of radiation from a distance?

A doctor is trained to evaluate the health of an individual by taking objective measurements. If you are not feeling well, the doctor may listen to your lungs, listen to your heart, examine your ear drum, examine your eyes, palpate your organs for firmness or sensitivity, check your reflexes, and take a blood sample. These days, medical tests are more refined so that the doctor need not be as hands-on with the patient. It is arguable whether this change has improved diagnostics and healthcare.

Brett Wade, PhD

Dr. Brett Says

- Often, when you see your doctor for a checkup, he or she is measuring aspects of your base frequency. He/she checks your pulse, your temperature, your reflexes, and feels for tension in your organs and muscle tone. All these measurements are a reflection of your overall base frequency. Reds tend to have slower reflexes than violets, who often have very brisk reflexes. Greens tend to have higher basal temperatures. At the Ekahi Health center, we do in-depth frequency profile which measure things like temperature, reflexes, and posture.

Before the advent of complex diagnostic tools such as X-rays, CT scans, and MRIs, a doctor's most effective and reliable diagnostic tool was his or her own senses. It was routine during an examination to smell the breath, observe and palpate the body, occasionally taste excretions such as urine, listen to the body, and listen to the person. A physician could tell a great deal about the health of a person by using his or her own five senses. In fact, the Ayurvedic physicians mentioned in chapter 3 were masters at evaluating subtle changes in a person. What made them particularly skillful was that they evaluated patients in states of relative health, not just when the patients were ill; the physicians' job was to keep them healthy.

Ayurvedic physicians determined which of three main doshas, or categories, a person fell into: kapha, pitta, or vata. They made this assessment based on observation and asking detailed questions about energy, sleep, diet, stress reactions, activity preference, and more. The Ayurvedic physician assessed the patient's pulse, urine, feces, tongue, strength of voice, skin sensation, vision, hearing, and body stature. With this information, the Ayurvedic physician determined diagnosis and treatment. The patient was then prescribed a healthy diet, exercise, and other lifestyle recommendations based on their dosha. The Ayurvedic diagnosis of unwellness related to an imbalance in the patient's dosha; the patient was said to have an excess or lack of their own dosha.

Dr. Brett Says

- The advent of technology has affected the intuitive skills of healthcare providers, impairing their abilities to detect subtle changes in patients. Since so many of our diagnostic and communication tools are electronic, we have become less adept at picking up on subtle cues from each other. It is likely that primitive man could detect pheromones and temperature changes in women and knew when she was ovulating. It is doubtful that most modern men could detect their partner's new hairstyle.

Since the time of Ayurveda, the original form of diagnostic medicine, physicians have relied less on their own senses and more on laboratory results. In fact, diagnosis can now be made while barely touching or speaking to a patient. It is not the fault of the physician, but of our modern world, which has embraced technology so quickly that more and more people rely on distant electronic communication rather than face-to-face contact. What do we lose when start to develop relationships online, or meet with coworkers electronically, or let physicians assess our health by reading lab reports? We miss picking up subtle frequencies. Our ancestors used to possess the ability to select a mate based on smell and certain visual characteristics that suggested a compatible match and healthy offspring. Many animals today still choose a mate based on subtle features and characteristics such as smell (Bhutta, 2007), but we modern humans have almost lost this important ability.

A recent study (Mujica-Parodi et al., 2009) showed that humans still have the ability smell fear in other humans. When we sweat, we release, among other things, pheromones. These are chemicals that have an effect on members of the same species. It has been suggested that our need to be hygienic and to wear artificial scents has masked our ability to detect pheromones as well as we should be able to. Nevertheless, the fact that humans can still detect fear pheromones suggests that we still possess the ability. Research has also shown that we are able to match the heart rate of a loved we see in distress. A recent study showed that when a person watches their loved one walk across hot coals, their heart rate synchronizes to the heart rate of the person walking the coals (Dell'Amore, 2011). We are definitely perceptive people. Now we need to learn how to hone our ability and master the waves of life.

Case Study

Mr. X was a college professor who taught first- and second-year chemistry classes. Students, colleagues, and anybody else who knew Mr. X would have described him as an affable, laid back, sensitive, and caring teacher. He had a colorful office with walls strewn with articles, papers, pictures, art, and anything that amused him. His red frequency class was a bit unusual in his field. He described most of his colleagues as Type A, overachievers, and competitive. When Mr. X was teaching, his frequency was generally well received by his students. On the other hand, at department meetings, his frequency was not appreciated. He often felt like the odd one out. Since he preferred to listen rather than to speak, he often found himself sitting in silence, yet not being able to convey his disagreement about some issues. More importantly, being around his colleagues drained him.

When I met Mr. X, he was still working at the college but had recently been diagnosed with a debilitating condition known as fibromyalgia. He was chronically fatigued and had diffuse pain all over his body. He also complained of headaches and inability to concentrate. His work was affected; teaching, which had once been his greatest joy, was becoming a real challenge. I could see immediately that Mr. X was red, but I had him complete a frequency profile to be certain. I was also able to determine that the majority of his colleagues were green, and some were blue. He explained that he met with his colleagues twice a month for a two-hour meeting.

I asked Mr. X when his symptoms began. He thought it had been approximately three years ago. I asked the usual questions about general health and conducted a thorough physical exam. He had classic fibromyalgia tender points on his body. He explained that three years ago a new Program Director (green) had been appointed and conducted a performance review. While Mr. X's teaching was not a concern, his new boss was concerned that he didn't appear to be a team player. To fit in, Mr. X tried to be more like his colleagues. He recalled actually changing his voice and mannerisms to more or less copy his colleagues. It did not surprise me to hear that this tactic actually worked. While his adjusted frequency was effective at work, it was affecting his health adversely.

I explained to Mr. X the toll his experiment had taken on his health. I told him that he had two choices: Learn to reset to base frequency every day, or find a new job. I taught him the importance of meditation and nourishing his red class. He followed my instructions and after three weeks there was noticeable improvement. His fatigue and pain were starting to improve. He now knows the power of adjusting his base frequency, but more importantly, he knows to *reset* every day.

In Summary

- Generally, all people of a base frequency class have some commonalities of body language.
- Once you learn to see different base frequencies in the public, you will start to become aware of the effects they have on your own waves.
- There are many different sources of nonionizing radiation that can be detected remotely in people.
- Our modern world has impaired our ability to detect waves from other people, but we can relearn it.
- If we are unaware of the effects that other people have on our base frequency, then our base frequency could be altered, which might eventually lead a disease to develop.

CHAPTER 7

What Is Electrosmog?

We do not inherit the earth from our ancestors; we borrow it from our children.
—Chief Seattle

In the previous chapter, we learned that people of different frequencies than ours can have a significant effect on our energy. Now we will learn about the effects of nonionizing, anthropogenic (man-made) sources of electromagnetic energy on our base frequency and our health. We will discuss the health effects of two parts of the nonionizing spectrum: *ultra high frequency* (UHF) and *extremely low frequency* (ELF) radiation. Most new communication technology operates in the microwave range of radio waves. This range of the spectrum is known as UHF and covers the range from 300 MHz to 3 GHz. ELF ranges from 3 Hz to 300 Hz and is the frequency at which all our wall appliances operate. ELF is also the frequency of overhead power lines (60 Hz).

Electrosmog is a relatively new term that describes invisible smog created by the recent explosion of wireless technology. When you use your cell phone, cordless phone, wireless router, baby monitor, garage door remote, television remote, radio; when your television or phone receives satellite signals; when your power meter transmits wireless signals; you are using nonionizing radiation. We cannot see these waves, but we know that they do something. Even if you yourself do not use wireless technology, you are living in the smog of these waves.

In chapter 2 we looked at the electromagnetic spectrum, a continuum of electrical and magnetic oscillating fields which run from ELF to high frequency (figure 4). While all these forms of radiation have been present in our atmosphere since the beginning of time, ever since man learned how radio waves could be used for communication, radiation from this part of the spectrum has exploded due to the number of devices now using these frequencies.

The ability to immediately access information and relay it to nearly any place on earth is mind-boggling. Marconi was arguably the father of wireless technology. Prior to sending his famous trans-Atlantic radio signal in 1900 from Signal Hill in St. John's, Newfoundland, he had been experimenting with communication that did not use wires. While wireless technology was not invented by Marconi, he is credited with commercializing and essentially operationalizing the work of physicists Faraday, Maxwell, Hertz, and Tesla.

Marconi's wireless telegraph was a piece of equipment that generated strong electrical currents and a resultant magnetic field which oscillated through the atmosphere and was received at a distant point by a receiver; this is essentially the way radio works today. In fact, cellular phones and Wi-Fi communication use essentially the same technology as Marconi's original invention! It is important to note that since the beginning of time, our universe has been exposed to all forms of radiation on the electromagnetic spectrum. The fact that we evolved in this soup of electromagnetic radiation means that we must have some natural immunity or protection from its potential negative health effects. We do have an amazing ability to be relatively unaffected by the frequencies of radiation which reach the surface of the earth.

Ultraviolet B radiation causes our skin to produce melanin, a pigment which tans our skin, and our pineal gland to produce melatonin, an important hormone involved in immunity and sleep. Infrared radiation provides us with warmth from convection heating. We can see because our retinas have evolved to see the frequencies of visible light. Radio waves that reach the earth from our sun and from cosmic sources likely have had no effect on us.

So why should we be concerned about the electrosmog if these frequencies are similar to those coming from the sun and from space? The reason for concern is that some of these devices are producing nonionizing radiation with levels of power that are much higher than what is naturally occurring. Cell phone towers, for example, use approximately 100 watts of power ("Human Exposure to Radio Frequency Fields: Guidelines For Cellular and PCS Sites," 2011). But the main reason for concern is that we cannot effectively account for spikes of high-intensity electromagnetic frequencies caused by constructive interference. When multiple sources of similar frequencies in our electrosmog come together, the waves can summate and create much higher ambient intensities.

These are some sources of UHF radiation in a typical home:

- wireless router
- baby monitor
- cordless phone
- cellular telephone
- Bluetooth wireless devices such as wireless keyboard or mouse
- microwave oven
- smart meter
- wireless security camera

Perhaps you remember the first generation of cordless phones with massive antennas in the 1980s. They operated at 1.7 MHz, and were discontinued because of security issues: it was too easy to eavesdrop on them. The frequencies have increased since then. Popular cordless phone frequencies now are 900 MHz, 1.9 GHz (Digital Enhanced Cordless Telecommunications - DECT), 2.4 GHz, and 5.8 GHz. The 2.4 GHz frequency is a crowded market (figure 18). Not only do many cordless phones operate at this frequency, but microwave ovens, many baby monitors, and most wireless routers and Wi-Fi technology do as well.

Figure 18. Common Sources of Nonionizing Radiation in the Microwave Range

Many Sources of Wireless Radiation at Similar Frequencies

At this point you may have noticed that microwave ovens, baby monitors, cordless phones, and cell phones can use the same frequency. You might also be wondering why a microwave oven needs a safety door yet phones and baby monitors don't. Before we get too paranoid, let's remind ourselves that waves of the same frequency can have different amplitudes and, therefore, different levels of power. Thankfully, the power levels of cordless phones and cell phones and baby monitors are nowhere close to the power of a microwave oven. Microwave ovens use up to 1000 W (watts) of power, whereas cordless phones use approximately 100 mW (milliwatts). You cannot get appreciable heat at 100 mW, but you can nuke your food at 1000 W (1,000,000 mW). In fact, the maximum power that a cell phone, baby monitor, or Wi-Fi or cordless phone is allowed to operate at is approximately 250 mW. Anybody who has used a cell phone or cordless phone for an extended periods knows there can be mild heating of the device, but it is generally believed that this is not enough heat to cause tissue damage.

The electrosmog environment is a soup of innumerable frequencies and intensities of electromagnetic radiation. When two similar frequencies come together, they summate, acting as wave amplifiers through constructive interference. Although limits have been established on our wireless equipment, the summative effect of wave amplification cannot be controlled. The federal governments of most developed nations manage bandwidth by leasing it. For example, the United States and Canada have specific frequencies that they lease to cell phone companies, other frequencies that they lease to radio corporations, and still other frequencies they lease to television broadcasters. There are also bandwidths reserved for military use, amateur radio broadcasting, emergency broadcasting, cordless phones, and many more specific uses. The volume of electrosmog in our environment boggles the mind!

Watts, Power Densities, and SAR

As mentioned at the beginning of this chapter, the two major contributors of electrosmog are ELF and UHF radiation. While both are nonionizing radiation, the intended purpose and generation of each is slightly different. Therefore, different units are used to measure their strength and the potential effects of absorption.

The most common sources of ELF are household wiring, transmission lines carrying electricity, and appliances or tools. To discuss the magnetic field strengths and limits of exposure of ELF, we use a measurement of microtesla or milligauss. This is the strength of the magnetic field surrounding the wire or appliance when it is turned on or when electricity is flowing.

UHF or microwave frequencies used for cellular telephones, wireless baby monitors, wireless routers, and cordless phones are different. Electromagnetic radiation (EMR) is not merely a consequence of using electricity; it is actually used in communication. When you use a cellular phone, a wireless signal of UHF electromagnetic waves travels between your phone and a cell phone tower. Your phone is actually a transmitter and a receiver of EMR. The EMR is carrying information which is then converted to sound or pictures.

Dr. Brett Says

- I realize that discussions about wireless communication can be mind boggling. My main intention is for you to understand the sheer volume of man-made wireless waves in your environment. These frequencies are all around you and passing through you. In addition to your cell phone, there are other sources: your neighbors' wireless routers, radio station frequencies, satellite signals, baby monitors, cordless phone signals, and many more. It is dizzying to think about all these wireless signals. I know your main concern is likely to be whether they cause you any harm. We will address that point in the next chapter.

Frequencies between 300 MHz to 3 GHz are needed to transmit the volume of information contained in wireless streaming video or music. Encoded bits of information in the form of a wave oscillate three hundred million to three billion times a second! By comparison, ELF radiation carries a frequency of 60 Hz—way too slow for our modern day communication needs.

The way UHF is measured is quite different to the way ELF is measured. First, there is the strength of the sending and receiving unit—for example, a wireless router in your home. This unit has a maximum allowable power output of approximately 4 W, although it generally uses far less. A watt is a unit measuring the rate at which energy is used. An appliance with a higher wattage uses energy more rapidly than one with a lower wattage. A 50-W light bulb will produce less light and less heat than a 100-W bulb. We can feel the amount of heat that radiates from a light bulb. Imagine if your wireless router used 100 watts? You might really feel some heat coming from that thing!

Wattage is an important factor in considering the production of wireless EMR signals, but the really important issue is how much radiation is absorbed by humans. Specific absorption rate (SAR) is the rate at which energy is absorbed in the body. It is measured in watts per kilogram (W/kg). Since it is difficult to measure the effects of absorption across the entire body, SAR levels are often based on research examining wattage per gram(s) of tissue. The United States Federal Communications Commission (FCC) and Health Canada have set a limit of 1.6 W/kg when averaged for 1 gram of tissue (La & German, 2012). The FCC limits cell phone towers to 500 W per channel ("Human Exposure to Radio Frequency Fields: Guidelines For Cellular and PCS Sites," 2011).

Dr. Brett Says

- It is easy to get lost in all the different measurements and limits of wireless communication. The main thing you need to understand is that while governments have set limits on the strength of wireless devices, it is impossible to control what happens when these waves interact with each other in our environment. We cannot account for constructive interference.

A device such as a wireless router in your home may operate at 100 to 200 mW, but if there are multiple similar frequencies of radiation travelling through your home, there is a possibility of spikes of higher, uncontrolled power are possible. Electrosmog is a soup of frequencies with unintended power spikes that could be a concern. Take a look back at figure 18—all these appliances and technologies add to the electrosmog. Now add to that radio waves, television satellite signals, smart meters, and overhead power lines, and you can see what a soup of frequencies we live in.

Extremely Low Frequency (ELF) Radiation

At the very end of those low-energy radio waves is a spectrum known as extremely low frequency (ELF) radiation (3-300 Hz). ELF radiation is emitted from sources such as appliances using 110 or 220 volts, current flowing through household wiring or overhead power lines, the sun, cosmic radiation sources, lightning strikes, and geomagnetic pulsations.

The following are some sources of ELF radiation in the home:

- magnetic fields from household wiring
- magnetic fields from appliances
- magnetic fields from overhead power lines or buried power lines

Magnetic field strengths in ELF radiation are measured in units called milligauss (mG), which is one-thousandth of a Gauss. Another unit is Tesla (T), which is 10,000 Gauss. The average magnetic field strength measured in a North American home is less than 2 mG (or 0.2 µT) ("EMF - Electric and Magnetic Fields Associated with the Use of Electric Power," 2002), but the strength of the magnetic field near some household appliances may be near 4000 mG (400 µT) ("Extremely Low Frequency Fields," 2007). The International Commission on Non-Ionizing Radiation (ICNIRP) has set maximum exposure levels of 2000 mG (200 µT) for the general public and 10,000 mG (1000 µT) for exposure at work ("Guidelines for limiting exposure to time-varying electric and magnetic fields (1 Hz to 100 kHz)," 2010).

Magnetic field strengths under or near overhead power lines (see table 5) are, in some cases, less than those of some appliances (see table 6). An appliance's magnetic field is only present when it is turned on; by contrast, the magnetic field of overhead power lines is relatively constant. This data about overhead power lines and appliances comes from the 2002 paper "EMF—Electric and Magnetic Fields Associated With the Use of Electric Power," which was the result of a significant project conducted by the National Institute of Environmental Health Sciences of the National Institutes of Health.

Table 5. Magnetic Field Strengths Near Overhead Power Lines

Type of overhead power lines	Average Magnetic Field Strengths (mG)			
	Directly under the line	50 feet	100 feet	200 feet
500 kV	86.7	29.4	12.6	3.2
230 kV	57.5	19.5	7.1	1.8
115 kV	29.7	6.5	1.7	0.4

Data From: ("EMF - Electric and Magnetic Fields Associated with the Use of Electric Power," 2002)

Table 6. Median Magnetic Field Exposures from Common Appliances

Appliance	Median magnetic field strength (mG)	
	At 6 inches	At 2 feet
Dishwasher	20	4
Blender	70	2
Electric range	30	2
Refrigerator	2	1
Toaster	10	nil
Baby monitor (transmitter)	6	nil
Washing machine	20	1
Portable electric heater	100	4
Electric clothes dryer	3	nil
Vacuum cleaner	300	10
Hair dryer	300	1
Fluorescent lights	40	2
Photocopiers	90	7

From: ("EMF - Electric and Magnetic Fields Associated with the Use of Electric Power," 2002)

Notice how dramatically the magnetic field strength drops both at distances from the power lines and distances from the appliances. At 2 feet, the magnetic field from most appliances is nil. Note that these are median measurements, which means that they are the middle measurements out of a range. The field strength of some appliances may be much higher than the median.

Average ELF Radiation Exposure in the Workplace

As mentioned, average home exposure is less than 2 mG, and the limits set for workplace exposure are 10,000 mG. Exposure levels for most occupations in North America are between 0.5 mG and 1 mG ("EMF - Electric and Magnetic Fields Associated with the Use of

Electric Power," 2002). Some industries, such as magnetic levitation train workers, welders, and electricians working on overhead power lines, may experience higher levels. The possible health effects of ELF and UHF exposure are discussed in more detail in the next chapter.

In Summary

- Electrosmog is a term which refers to the soup of nonionizing radiation frequencies all around us from sources such as cell phone towers, wireless routers, baby monitors, wireless alarms, and remote controls.
- While most countries have limits on the intensities of radiation sources (SAR levels), we cannot account for the mixing of waves and the potential for constructive interference.
- Extremely Low Frequency (ELF) radiation and Ultra High Frequency (UHF) radiation easily pass through human tissue.
- Sources of ELF radiation include appliances, household wiring, and overhead power lines.
- Sources of UHF radiation include baby monitors, cordless phones, wireless routers, and cellular telephones.

CHAPTER 8

Effects of Electrosmog on Base Frequency and Health

> *Sensitivity to electromagnetic radiation is the emerging health problem of the 21st century. It is imperative health practitioners, governments, schools and parents learn more about it. The human health stakes are significant.*
> —William Rea, MD

In the previous chapter, we learned what electrosmog is and about the limits suggested for ELF and UHF radiation. Now we are going to look at how these frequencies might affect our own base frequency and our health.

As we discussed in the last chapter, while limits on the maximum amount of radiation deemed to be safe for human exposure have been set, it is impossible to account for the effects of constructive interference: spike in wave amplitudes. Research has suggested that it is pulsed (on for a short time and then off for a short time), not continuous fields that have the most biological effect (Panagopoulos, Karabarbounis, & Margaritis, 2002).

The question of whether electrosmog (wireless UHF waves and/or ELF waves), affects health is a controversial one. Before we delve into this quagmire, we need to understand how health research is conducted. Most health research that examines possible effects falls into the following three broad categories:

Table 7. Comparison of Health Research

In vitro: Studying cells in a petri dish	*In vivo:* Studying effects on the entire body
Experimental: Comparing the effects on a group receiving treatment or exposure to a control group	*Nonexperimental:* Statistical analysis of existing data
Human: Studying human cells, tissues, organs, systems, or whole body	*Animal:* Studying animal cells, tissues, organs, systems, or whole body

Much of the health research on ELF are in vitro, human, or animal studies. The reason you see very little experimental research on humans is that a research study that intentionally exposes humans to magnetic field intensities that may have negative health effects would be unethical and unlikely to be approved by any research ethics board. UHF research is also commonly nonexperimental; researchers study available data and look for correlations and calculate risk ratios.

Extremely Low Frequency (ELF) Radiation Health Effects

So, what effect could an invisible magnetic field generated by a 110V-source at 60 Hz (50 Hz in Europe) possibly have on humans? The majority of health research on the potential effects of exposure to ELF fields has looked at the relationship between disease and exposure to overhead power lines and household wiring. As electrons move through these wires, an invisible magnetic field is generated. Since the electrons are contained in the wire, their effects are easily mitigated. The World Health Organization has concluded that "there are no substantive health concerns related to electric fields at levels generally encountered by the public" ("Electromagnetic fields and public health," 2007). It is the effects of the magnetic field which are of concern. Magnetic field lines radiate out from wires and easily penetrate walls, floors, and most other household constructions. As you can imagine, they pass easily through us, too. Let's now take a look at some selected research which has found health effects from ELF.

Table 8. Selected Research Showing Health Effects from ELF Exposure Studies

Reference	Intensities	Type of Study	Effects
(Ivancsits, Pilger, Diem, Jahn, & Rudiger, 2005)	Pulsed 50 Hz, 1 mT for 1-24 hours	*In vitro*	DNA damage in two types of humans cells and one type of rat cell
(Antonopoulos, Yang, Stamm, Heller, & Obe, 1995)	50 Hz; 5 mT	*In vitro*	Increased cell dividing rate of lymphocytes
(Ivancsits, Diem, Pilger, Rudiger, & Jahn, 2002)	50 Hz, sinusoidal, 24 h, 1000 µT	*In vitro*	DNA damage in human fibrocytes
(Seyhan & Canseven, 2006)	50 Hz, 0.2 mT-3 mT	*In vivo animal*	Some cells or tissues affected: collagen synthesis, antioxidant defense system, and immune cells
(Winker, Ivancsits, Pilger, Adlkofer, & Rudiger, 2005)	50 Hz, sinusoidal, 5'-field-on/10'-field-off, 2-24 h, 1 mT	*In vitro*	Evidence of chromosome damage after ten hours
(Wolf et al., 2005)	24-72 h to 0.5-1.0 mT 50 Hz	*In vitro*	Evidence of DNA damage after twenty-four hours in three types of cells

(Cook, Thomas, Keenliside, & Prato, 2005)	ELF for 15 minutes at 200 μT	*In vivo* human EEG brain waves	After fifteen minutes of exposure, significant decrease in alpha brain wave activity
(Bianchi et al., 2000)	Twenty cases examined for relationship between childhood leukemia and proximity to power lines	*Correlation*	Fourfold increase in childhood leukemia for homes with high background magnetic field strength
(Draper, Vincent, Kroll, & Swanson, 2005)	29,081 cancer cases examined for background magnetic field exposure living near power lines (50 Hz)	*Correlation*	Relative risk of 1.69 (low risk) for developing cancer if living within two hundred meters of power lines

It is important to note that the studies in table 8 are selected studies which show an effect from exposure to ELF. There is also a significant volume of research which contradicts these findings, which is why the World Health Organization (WHO) has deemed that exposure to ELF poses no significant health risk.

While the selected studies suggest significant health effects from ELF such as DNA damage and childhood leukemia, a closer inspection of these studies should give us comfort; the effects, if any, are minimal. In in vitro studies, specific cells in a petri dish are exposed to a treatment of, in this case, ELF or UHF. The results of in vitro studies cannot be extrapolated to the full body. The human body has not only layers of protective tissue, but also an immune system that is well-equipped to deal with DNA damage, cell damage, and free-radical production. It is also important to realize that correlation is *not* the same as causation. In other words, just because two variables are positively linked—for example, as exposure increases, so do harmful health effects—does not mean that one causes the other. This said, the fact that some research (such as the studies listed above) does demonstrate positive effects is enough motivation for me to minimize the chronic exposure to the magnetic fields from ELF when it is reasonable to do so. We will look at strategies for mitigation, or harm reduction, of both ELF and UHF later in this chapter.

Important Point

- "Positive effects" means that as either intensity or exposure time increases, so does the rate of harmful effects.
- Just because a positive relationship exists does not mean that increased exposure time or intensity causes disease. It is just a relationship. The positive effect could be the result of other unaccounted-for variables like age, health, occupation, genetics, etc.
- Chronic exposure means exposure for long periods of time. In many cases, this is years of exposure. Chronic exposure might be a factor in a house or workplace if a person has been there for many years.

Extremely Low Frequency (ELF) Radiation Health Effects

If research does support some possible health effects (albeit weak or in vitro), what are the possible mechanisms? We know that magnetic field strengths in most homes are not strong enough to cause DNA damage, nor to be ionizing. The following are some theories as to how ELF could contribute to health effects or disease.

The Ion Theory: This theory states that ELF fields have the ability to cause ions, either free ions or those attached to cell membranes (for example, sodium, potassium, calcium), to allow more ions to enter cell and organelles (little parts in the cells), and that this could affect the cells' metabolism. That means that some cells would increase or decrease in metabolism, which is the rate at which they make important things like DNA or proteins.

Magnetic Induction Theory: This theory is that ELF magnetic fields induce an electric field by causing ions to move. This electric field is thought to possibly alter physiology and thus be a contributor to disease.

Voltage-gated channel theory: This theory suggests that magnetic fields create little gates in cell membranes; when there is a voltage change, these gates are stimulated to open or close.

Free radical theory: Numerous animal studies have found that there is an increase in free radical production with exposure to ELF.

If any or all of these theories are correct, then external ELF could theoretically affect cellular metabolism and, therefore, affect the rate at which cells not only divide but also produce proteins, energy, and hormones such as melatonin. If a cells' ability to produce hormones such as melatonin is affected, this could lead eventually to disease. It appears that ELF waves might be related to disease, but through complex and subtle effects that are likely tertiary.

Ultra High Frequency (UHF) Radiation Health Effects

As with ELF radiation, UHF radiation does not possess enough energy to be ionizing. Moreover, neither frequency appears to have sufficient energy to cause significant heating (except at extremely high powers). Recall that the main sources of UHF radiation are wireless signals used for communication such as cell phone signals, television signals, and wireless routers. Its potential health effects have recently become a major focus of research; over five billion people in the world use cell phones. Add to this claims of a relationship between cell phone usage and brain cancer.

If UHF radiation does not heat or ionize (it does not carry enough power to dislodge an electron), then what could be the mechanism for health effects? It is likely that, as with ELF, most purported health effects are tertiary and related to nonionizing radiation, and that effects are not immediate or necessarily obvious. Here are some selected studies which have shown positive effects.

Dr. Brett Says

- And now to address the concern about whether or not cell phones cause cancer: In the next table I will show you some selected studies that demonstrate, in some cases, a positive correlation between cell phone use and brain cancer. I remind you again of the important fact that correlation does not equal causation. In other words, just because two variables are related doesn't mean that one causes the other. Another important point is that while the evidence of causation may not currently be present, the technology (cell phones) is very new.

Table 9. Selected Positive Effects from UHF Exposure Studies

Reference	Intensities or study design	Type of Study	Effects
(Lehrer, Green, & Stock, 2011)	Cell phone contracts in 19 states compared with brain cancer rates	Correlation	"There was a significant correlation between number of cell phone subscriptions and brain tumors in nineteen US states ($r = 0.950$, $P < 0.001$)"

(Volkow Nd & et al., 2011)	To determine if fifty minutes of cell phone use cause an increase in brain metabolism	In vivo, PET scan of brain	Metabolism in the region closest to the antenna was significantly higher for on than for off conditions
(Khurana, Teo, Kundi, Hardell, & Carlberg, 2009)	Meta-analyses to determine if long-term cell phone use (≥10 years) is related to cancer. 11 studies analyzed	Meta-analysis	"The results indicate that using a cell phone for ≥10 years approximately doubles the risk of being diagnosed with a brain tumor on the same side (ipsilateral) of the head as that preferred for cell phone use. The data achieve statistical significance for glioma and acoustic neuroma but not for meningioma"
(Hocking, Gordon, Grain, & Hatfield, 1996)	Ecological study to calculate risk ratio for cancer incidence	Risk ratio calculation	"For all ages, the rate ratio for total leukemia incidence was 1.24. Among children, the rate ratio for leukemia incidence was 1.58 and for mortality it was 2.32. The rate ratio for childhood lymphatic leukemia was 1.55 for incidence and 2.74 for mortality"
(Hillert et al., 2008)	Study of cell phone use and headaches	Double-blind, cross-over	Headaches more common in cell phone exposure group
(Divan, Kheifets, Obel, & Olsen, 2008)	Questionnaire on cell phone use and behavioral questionnaire	Calculation of odds ratio	"Exposure to cell phones prenatally—and, to a lesser degree, postnatally—was associated with behavioral difficulties such as emotional and hyperactivity problems around the age of school entry"

As with the ELF studies, the selected UHF studies (table 9) demonstrate a positive relationship (i.e. an increase) between UHF exposure and diseases such as cancer. As with ELF, the risk ratios are generally weak or they are merely correlations that cannot suggest causation. Research which shows correlations between cell phones and brain cancer is starting to mount. It is important to realize that mechanisms such as increased brain cell metabolism and increased free radical production are going to have tertiary and relatively slow effects. This is something to be aware of since this technology is not only new, but also exploding in use.

Recently, a working group of thirty-one scientists from fourteen different countries, as part of the WHO's International Agency for Research on Cancer (IARC), met to discuss the findings of all the available scientific research related to cell phones and cancer. The group decided to classify cell phone use as "possibly carcinogenic." This Group 2B rating is similar to the risk category of lead exposure, chloroform, and coffee consumption. These findings and the IARC classification have led some European nations to investigate ways to limit personal radio frequency exposure.

Since the free radical theory is purported to be a mechanism of diseases related to ELF and UHF, it is important to remind ourselves what free radicals are and how they are related to disease.

Free Radicals

The term *free radical* is used rather loosely by lay people in discussing health matters. First, it is important to note that free radicals are neither good nor bad; in fact, they are vital. Free radicals are atoms or molecules that have lost an electron from their outer shell. Actually, it was not lost, but forcefully removed in a chemical reaction. In fact, most free radicals are produced naturally as our bodies produce energy. In a beautiful process called cellular respiration, our cells use oxygen to produce energy in the mitochondria, an organelle. Energy in the form of the molecule adenosine triphosphate (ATP) is produced using sugar and oxygen. Carbon dioxide (CO^2) and water (H_2O) are produced as waste products.

In addition to energy (ATP), CO^2, and H_2O, reactive oxygen species (ROS) such as O^{2-} are produced. Since ROS like O^{2-} have donated an electron, they have the ability to bind with other atoms or molecules and to create a cascade effect of atoms or molecules being stripped of an electron. This might not sound too bad, but if the ROS strips an electron from DNA or proteins in the body, it can affect genetics and lead to disease. While our bodies do produce free radicals such as O^{2-} naturally, levels of these ROS species can rise precipitously when our bodies are exposed to environmental toxins such as cigarette smoke, pollution, electrosmog, ionizing radiation, and diets high in saturated fats.

Fortunately, the body also counter effect these naturally occurring free radicals. The body produces chemicals such as glutathione, which readily combine with ROS and effective neutralize them by reducing them. These chemicals are known as antioxidants. We will further discuss antioxidants at the end of the chapter when we discuss mitigation strategies for ELF and UHF.

Effects of ELF and UHF on Base Frequency

Now we know that ELF and UHF may have health effects related to free radical production, ion effects, and cellular metabolism changes. We also know that the Ekahi Method is all about waves, both your own and external ones. We have discussed electrosmog and the sources of this soup of external frequencies. How might Electrosmog affect our own base frequency?

In my years of treating patients and using the Ekahi Method frequency profile, I have noticed that electrosmog is definitely related to health. Since numerous studies have shown that external magnetic fields, including alterations of the earth's magnetic field, can affect heart rate (Chernouss, Vinogradov, & Vlassova, 2001; Sait, Wood,

& Sadafi, 1999; Sastre, Cook, & Graham, 1998), it is conceivable that electrosmog could pull people out of their base frequency. In treating patients, I have noticed that some people appear to be more sensitive to this effect than others. These people, known as the electromagnetically sensitive, appear susceptible to physiological effects related to ELF and UHF.

I believe that for many people, if not for everyone, *electrosmog is a potential uncontrolled wave reducer*. Because of its high-frequency pulsations (most wireless technology is pulsed), it creates aberrant waves and may pull us out of base frequency. I have no proof of this, but I do know that since UHF exposure can immediately affect heart rate (Havas et al., 2010), it stands to reason that it can pull you out of base frequency; all the more reason for us to regularly reset to base frequency.

Case Study

> Mr. S came to see me after one of my talks. He was a middle-aged man, recently divorced and suffering from depression. He was taking medication, but his symptoms of depression had been progressively getting worse for the past five years. As is common with depression, he also complained of fatigue and general body pain. I asked him questions about his health and determined that besides his depression, he was a healthy man. I determined that his base frequency was green. It was clear that he was out of balance. His body language and rate of speech had initially made me think he was violet.
>
> I needed to understand what was causing him to be so out of balance. He had an office job in which he worked on a computer all day. He did very little exercise and spent little time outdoors. His leisure time was spent

watching television and surfing the internet. I asked about his sleeping environment and he reported that he had recently moved into a rented basement suite with a small bedroom. He mentioned that he had trouble sleeping due to the background hum of an electrical panel. In fact, the head of his bed was directly beneath 200-amp breaker.

I asked if he would try an experiment for me. He agreed to move his bed into his living room and try sleeping there. I decided not to add any other changes or variables to the experiment at that time. Three weeks later, he came back to see me with a smile on his face. The only change he had made was to move his bed away from a strong magnetic field. He almost immediately started to sleep better and his mental health improved significantly. Next, I had him start exercising regularly outside and start taking melatonin (a powerful antioxidant).

I saw Mr. S. several months later when we were both out jogging. I did not recognize him at first. He was confident, happy, energetic and back to his green self.

Limiting Exposure to High Levels of ELF and UHF

The good news is that we can limit our exposure to high levels of ELF and UHF. There are effective ways to limit your exposure to the ELF magnetic field coming from appliances and wiring and to the wireless sources of UHF. The most effective method is with *distance*. If you look back at the previous chapter you can see that just by moving a small distance away from the source of ELF (wires, appliances, electrical panels) or UHF (wireless routers, baby monitors, cell phones, cordless phones), you can dramatically decrease the intensity of the field.

The inverse square law states that the intensity of a radiated source is inversely proportional to the square of the distance. This means that doubling the distance from radiating source cuts results to a quarter of their original intensity. In other words, moving from one foot away to two feet away means you now are exposed to a quarter of the intensity. If, at one foot from a source such as a wireless router, the strength was 1 $\mu W/cm^2$, then at two feet, you would have 0.25 $\mu W/cm^2$. Distance does matter!

This important mitigation technique can be applied to all electromagnetic waves. So for both ELF and UHF, the most important thing that you can do to minimize exposure to these fields is to move further away. Even a few feet makes a big difference.

Dr. Brett's Top Five Easily Mitigated ELF Sources

1) *Clock radio*: Most people I know have one of these in their bedroom. Magnetic field measures approximately 50 mG (5 µT) right next to the clock but drops to 0.6 mG (0.06 µT) at two feet away. Get your clock radio away from your head! Move it at least two feet away—it may prevent you from whacking the snooze button and get you out of bed.
2) *Hair dryer*: 130 mG (13.0 µT), aimed at your head! Granted, hair dryers are not usually on for long periods, but perhaps consider using a towel instead. Please do not blow dry your kids' hair.
3) *Electric razor*: 2230 mG (223 µT) again, very close to the brain. Yes, it is only used for short periods. Yes, I know how expensive razor blades are. But beards are stylish at the moment!
4) *Microwave oven*: 470 mG (47 µT). No, microwaves will not kill you, nor do they make the food you eat radioactive.

However, do not put your head near the microwave when it is running. Stand three feet back and you will be fine.

5) *Transformers*: 30 mG-150 mG (3 µT-15 µT). These are the small black boxes that you plug into the wall to power many appliances such as laptops, portable DVD players, cordless-phone base stations, printers, computer speakers, baby monitors, routers, game systems, etc. Their purpose is to transform alternating current of 110 V from the plug into direct current of a smaller voltage. Keep transformers at least three feet away from your heads when you're asleep.

Before we examine mitigation tips for UHF, we need to define some frequently used language related to microwave radio frequency. With ELF, we are essentially looking at the strength of the magnetic field measured in either mG or µT. The International Commission on Non-Ionizing Radiation Protection (ICNIRP) has set a general public exposure limit of 2,000 mG (200 µT), and Health Canada and the FCC have set a SAR limit of 1.6 W/kg for UHF. The other term you will see regularly is *power density*. Power density is a measurement of power over a unit of area. Measurements of the power density from a radiated source such as a cell phone are usually in microwatts per centimeter squared ($\mu W/cm^2$). While there are no limits per se to power density, the higher the power density is, the higher the SAR level.

Dr. Brett's Top Five Easily Mitigated UHF Sources

1) *Cell phone*: 1,000-5,000 $\mu W/cm^2$ at ear. SAR levels* range from 0.3 W/kg to 2.0 W/kg. Yes, I have a smart phone and yes, I love it. However, I rarely make calls on my cell phone. If I have to make a call that will last more than a couple of minutes, I look for a landline or I simply text. Texting gets that UHF away from your head. When I do use my phone for a conversation, I use the speakerphone or hold the phone away from my head. Even a few inches make a big difference!

2) *Baby monitor*: 2.9 µW/cm. SAR levels* range from 0.01 W/kg to 0.08 W/kg. Yes, the SAR level is low, but if you have it on all the time, a baby might be exposed fourteen to sixteen hours a day. Get that thing away from your child! It works just fine several feet away. You can get wired versions of these devices, as well as voice-activated, which is better as it is not on all the time. Avoid DECT baby monitors, which use more power. Some baby monitors may operate with power up to 500 mW.

3) *Wireless router*: 0.2-1.0 µW/cm^2. It is difficult to find published data on SAR levels*. I love Ethernet cables, but I realize that it is a pain to run cables all over your house. I should know, as I have pulled Ethernet cables though my sixty-year-old house for fifteen separate jacks! If you must use a router, make sure it is at least three feet away from where you sleep.

4) *Cordless phones that use DECT technology*: 205 µW/cm^2 at the phone. SAR level* of DECT phones: 0.01 W/kg and 0.05 W/kg DECT technology uses high power (up to 500 mW) and is on continuously. Consider non-DECT cordless phones (approximately 5 µW/cm^2). You can still buy corded phones that have answering machines.

5) *Wireless function in a laptop computer or tablet*: SAR levels*: 1.04 W/kg. It is hard to find published SAR levels for laptops and tablets, but they are similar to cell phones. If you can, turn off the wireless function.

* FCC limits and Health Canada SAR limits are 1.6 W/kg

Dr. Brett Says

- Again, I know that all the different measurements, from ELF (µT and mG) to UHF, SAR levels (W/kg), and power densities (µW/cm^2) can be confusing. The most important thing to keep in mind is that research does not yet support claims of ELF or UHF causing disease. However, there is a mounting body of research that may start to tip the scales one day. There are mechanisms which explain how ELF and UHF could contribute to disease. If you are concerned, use the inverse square law and move away from the source!

Additional Protection Tips

- Consider taking melatonin supplements at night. Melatonin is a powerful antioxidant.
- Make sure your diet is loaded with antioxidants (see chapter 15).
- Get a good night's sleep every night. Make sure your bedroom is dark; reduce or eliminate all light sources.
- If your bed is close to an electrical panel or immovable sources of ELF and UHF, try to move your bed to a new spot.
- Don't use electric blankets.
- Try not to have extension cords behind or under your bed
- Maintain safe distances (at least two feet) from televisions and computer screens.

In Summary

- Research does show some cellular and physiological changes in humans and animals exposed to ELF and UHF.
- There are mechanisms which may explain some of these positive results. One of these mechanisms is an increase in free radical production.
- While only selected positive studies were shown in this chapter, there are numerous studies that find no effect in vitro or in vivo from exposure to ELF and UHF.

- Since it has been shown that ELF and UHF exposure can alter heart rate, the Ekahi Method views overexposure to ELF and UHF as potential factors that could alter base frequency.
- Most countries have set limits to ELF and UHF exposure. These limits require appliance manufacturers using ELF or UHF to comply.
- Some people might be electromagnetically sensitive and thus be more affected by ELF and UHF.
- The easiest way to limit exposure to ELF and UHF is to increase your distance from the source. A good rule of thumb is to be at least three feet from appliances and wireless emitters. This is very important in rooms where you spend a lot of time like the bedroom.

PART III
Reset to Base Frequency

CHAPTER 9

Being Out of Base Frequency

A genius is the one most like himself.
—*Thelonious Monk*

We have learned in previous chapters how people and even nonliving sources of waves, such as those from electrosmog, can have dramatic effects on our own *base frequency*. How do you know when you are not in your base frequency? While some people might go out of their base frequency for a few hours and then return, others might remain unnaturally out of their frequency for days, months, or even years.

The following are some subtle things you might notice if you are not in your base frequency:

- elevated blood pressure
- rapid, shallow breathing
- difficulty sleeping
- changes in weight
- excessive changes in circulation in the hands or feet or excess sweating
- headaches
- increased tension in neck and shoulders
- difficulty concentrating

- changes in appetite
- changes in libido

If you think these changes seem like the symptoms of somebody who is stressed, you are correct! A major contributor to stress and disease is being out of your base frequency for too long.

Dr. Brett Says

- Many people are surprised when they learn what their base frequency is. When people don't know what their natural frequency is, they often live in the frequency they think they should be, not what they actually are. When you know your base frequency, you know what it feels like to be out of balance. The Ekahi Method believes that all disease is related to being chronically out of base frequency.

What Is *Balance*?

In chapters 2 and 3, we talked about wave frequency (the number waves in a second) and amplitude (the height of the wave). We also discussed the importance of constructive and destructive interference. Not only can our base frequency be pulled to higher or lower frequencies, we can also experience tremendous flattening or unnatural elevation of the amplitude of our wave. We talked about wave reducers and wave amplifiers and the importance of finding the natural zone on your wave. The natural zone is the range of energy within your base frequency that is not too high and not too low. We must realize that it is natural to cycle up and down on your wave.

Being in *balance* is the healthful state of you being in your base frequency and naturally cycling up and down in amplitude in your natural zone. You know you are in balance when you feel well and your energy naturally cycles through the day. If your base frequency is red, you would be in balance if your energy was slow at the start of the day, built at midday and came down in late afternoon, and then cycled back up through the evening before coming back down before bed.

Important Point

- Your base frequency can be forced to adopt a different frequency by any of the following four things:
  1. Subconsciously adopting somebody else's base frequency
  2. Purposely adjusting your base frequency to suit an environment or person
  3. Exposure to unrelenting and uncontrolled wave reducers and wave amplifiers
  4. Exposure to an unrelenting environment of discordant frequencies (like electrosmog)

Described below are the balanced energy cycles for each base frequency class over the course of a day. The bottom axis of each graph denotes the twenty-four-hour clock. Most energy cycles begin between 5:00 and 8:00, and end before 24:00. The other axis is an arbitrary scale of energy running from 0 to 5. These graphs are similar to the ones we saw in chapter 5 illustrating the natural zone, riding too low, and riding too high. The following graphs in this chapter all depict typical natural zones.

Red Frequency Class Energy Cycle

People in red frequency class tend to prefer waking up slowly and often will naturally sleep until nine in the morning. They have good energy throughout the day with a midafternoon lull in energy. They often regain their energy in late afternoon and then carry it through the late evening.

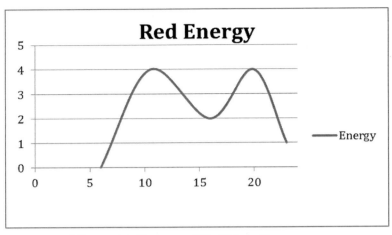

Figure 19. Energy of Red Base Frequency

Yellow Frequency Class Energy Cycle

People in yellow frequency have a distinctive bimodal distribution of their energy. They tend to start slowly and naturally wake around eight o'clock but reach their morning peak around ten. They have a decrease in energy around two but peak again around six before their energy tails off around nine o'clock.

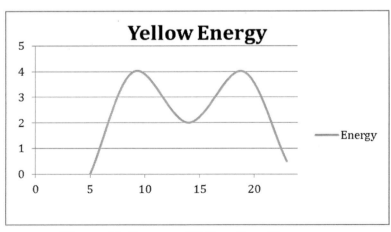

Figure 20. Energy of Yellow Base Frequency

Green Frequency Class Energy Cycle

People in green frequency class tend to wake up naturally before seven in the morning and reach peak energy by eight. They have a slight dip in energy around noon, but regain their energy by approximately one. Their energy quickly tails off around five o'clock.

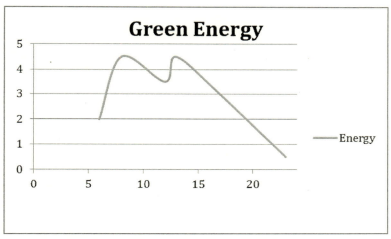

Figure 21. Energy of Green Base Frequency

Blue Frequency Class Energy Cycle

People of blue frequency class wake up naturally before seven and reach their morning peak by eight. They have a slight dip in energy around ten o'clock but regain it quickly by noon. Then their energy declines slowly until five, when it drops precipitously.

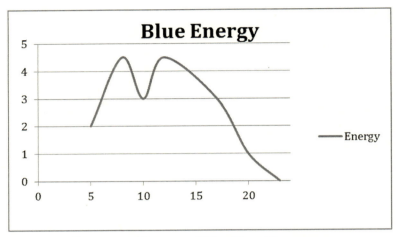

Figure 22. Energy of Blue Base Frequency

Violet Frequency Class Energy Cycle

People in violet frequency class tend to wake up naturally around six o'clock or earlier. Their energy peaks by seven and then drops around nine. They have another peak around eleven and another drop around one. They have one more peak around three o'clock before their energy drops precipitously for the day. They go through their day with short bursts of energy and tire easily.

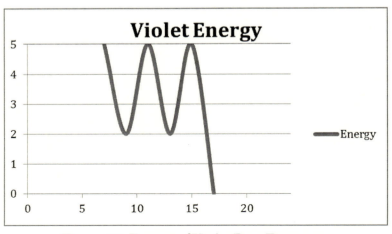

Figure 23. Energy of Violet Base Frequency

An Exercise

The previous graphs and descriptions of base frequency are based on observations and interviews with people from each class. The cycles may not accurately reflect your own typical energy in a day. On the following graph, draw your cycles over a typical day from the time you wake until the time you fall asleep. Start the scale on the horizontal axis at 5:00 (5:00 a.m.) and end it at 20:00 (8:00 p.m.). The scale on the vertical axis (0-5) represents your energy, with 5 being maximum energy. Do you have daily fluctuations? When does your energy drop? Remember that this is a normal cycle during periods of stable health.

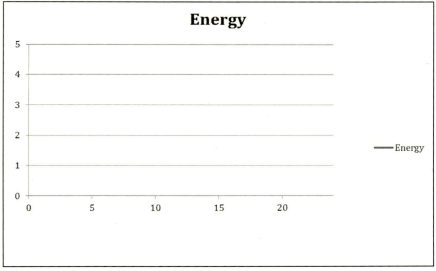

Figure 24. Your Energy in a Day

Knowing your energy cycle in the natural zone can help you best plan your activities. It is useful information to share if you are in a long-term relationship so that your partner can respect your natural rhythms. The following table contains some descriptors that are fairly typical for each base frequency when a person of that class is out of balance.

Table 10. Out-of-Balance Descriptors

	Physical Energy	Emotions or Mood	Social Interaction	Sleep	Eating and Digestion
Red	Sluggish, lethargic, intolerant of cold and damp.	Sad, quiet, melancholic, broody, hypersensitive, cantankerous.	Withdrawn, reluctant to speak or communicate, turning inward. Extreme intolerance of others in space and environment.	Increased need for sleep, tired, tending to stay up late and sleep late. May have insomnia.	Stop eating regular meals. May eat for comfort.
Yellow	Unproductive, aloof, less tolerant of cold and damp.	Sulky, sullen, critical, prickly, huffy, mercurial.	More withdrawn, moody, tending to be sarcastic and mocking of others. Impatient with others in space.	Tired and "foggy." Tending to stay up later and sleep later. Increased need for naps during day.	Eat more than usual and less healthy choices. Drawn to salty and fatty foods.
Green	Apathetic, spiritless, overheated.	Irritable, recalcitrant, snappish, mean, volatile.	Talking aggressively, impatient with others, tending to snap at others. Unpredictable with those in space.	Wanting to go to bed earlier. Desire frequent naps.	Increased snacking and fewer healthy, well-balanced meals. Increased snacking on sweet foods.
Blue	Discouraged, pessimistic, feeling cold and chilled.	Distracted, unpredictable, erratic, capricious, inconsistent, easily upset, high-strung.	Reaching out to others, speech louder and more impatient, easily exasperated and frustrated with others. Want people around but may be thorny with them.	Feeling increased need for sleep, but sleep is fitful. Not refreshed upon waking.	Increased eating of foods such as cakes and cookies. Increased complaints of digestive problems. Tendency toward constipation.

| Violet | Restless, frenetic, moving quickly from one task to another but ineffective productivity. Cold hands and feet. | Extremely anxious and keyed-up, uptight, neurotic. May be prone to anger quickly, quick to upset. | Reaching out to others, seem panicky. Extreme need to talk; decreased ability to listen. Curt and snippy. Want people around but can't connect. | Sleeping less, agitated during sleep, difficult to settle. | Difficulty eating. Food causes digestive upset. May eat more candies and chocolate. Prone to constipation. |

An Exercise

What words describe how you feel when you are out of balance (out of your base frequency and/or natural zone)? Write four or five words in each column.

Table 11. Your Out-of-Balance Descriptors

	Physical Energy	Emotions or Mood	Social Interaction	Sleep	Eating and Digestion
Your Base Frequency: _____					

Case Study

Recently, I had a family member complete the frequency profile. I asked her to do so because she seemed to be living a life that wasn't really for her. I felt she was a red trying to live the life of a green. She had some problems with sleeping and high blood pressure. When she completed the profile we found she was indeed a red base frequency. Her body language suggested to me that she was trying to be a green. Her job was in management. She was the only female in the office and a staff of fifteen men reported to her. She felt that in order to be respected, she needed to adopt a higher frequency at work. While this had likely been effective at work, she never practiced resetting, and as such, she had spent the last twenty years of her life living out of her base frequency.

While I was not sure that having her practice resetting every day would improve her symptoms of unrestful sleep and high blood pressure, it certainly couldn't hurt to try. She started to practice meditation regularly and learned to really honor her red base frequency. She nourished it with activities and foods that felt right for her. After just two weeks, she noticed that she was sleeping better and that her blood pressure was coming down. She still takes medications for her blood pressure, but she is now sleeping soundly through the night.

At this point you should have some idea of what it feels like to be out of balance. It is important to get in touch with these feelings because they will indicate to you that you may be out of your base frequency. In the next chapter, we will learn the most important way to reset back to our base frequency and allowing normalization and flow of our natural energy. In part 5 of the book, we will learn to maintain our base frequency and natural flow of energy by surrounding ourselves with resonant frequencies and environments.

In Summary

- You can be moved out of your natural base frequency by (1) subconsciously adopting somebody else's base frequency, (2) purposely adjusting your base frequency to suit an environment or person, (3) exposure to unrelenting and uncontrolled

wave reducers and wave amplifiers, and (4) exposure to an unrelenting environment of discordant frequencies (like electrosmog).
- When we are out of base frequency, we will notice changes in our physiology and our health.
- It is important to know what it feels like to be out of balance so that you know when you need to reset to base frequency.
- Your goal is to learn to reset to base frequency and learn what it is like to cycle through the full amplitude of your wave on a daily basis.
- Each base frequency has typical energy cycles throughout the day—these must be respected.
- Trying to live in a base frequency that is not natural can lead to disease.

CHAPTER 10

Resetting to Base Frequency

The best cure for the body is a quiet mind.
—Napoleon Bonaparte

We have learned that our *base frequency* can get pushed or pulled around by a variety of external forces such as other people or man-made sources of electromagnetic radiation (ELF and UHF). Remember, your base frequency can be moved out of your natural frequency by (1) subconsciously adopting somebody else's base frequency, (2) purposely adjusting your base frequency to suit an environment or person, (3) exposure to unrelenting and uncontrolled wave reducers and wave amplifiers, and (4) exposure to unrelenting environment of discordant frequencies (like electrosmog).

I have shown you with some case studies how being pulled out of your base frequency and staying out of it for too long can be not only fatiguing, but in the long term, possibly hazardous to your health. The previous chapter provided you with some simple ways to determine whether you are out of your base frequency. Now we will learn the cornerstone of the Ekahi Method: resetting to base frequency through *meditation*.

There are many different types of meditation, but they focus essentially on centering and inducing a state of relaxation. In the

Ekahi Method, we use meditation to get in touch with our base frequency. By practicing meditation, we reset to our base frequency and learn to feel our waves. The Ekahi Method has two optional tools to assist with meditation: scents and meditation beads. I will describe how these are used later in the chapter.

Meditation has been around for thousands of years. As I described in chapter 3, Ayurveda is an ancient form of medicine. Its earliest writings are in the Vedas, ancient Hindu texts written in Sanskrit approximately between 1000 and 1500 BC. Meditation as a practice of spiritual enlightenment or seeking a closer connection with God began to flourish around 600 to 500 BC in China as part of Taoism and in India as part of Buddhism. The Silk Road helped the Buddhist practice of meditation spread throughout the Mediterranean countries of Europe. There is evidence that meditation was a part of early Judaism; its origins are discussed in the Torah (Genesis 24:63).

Throughout the middle ages, the practice of meditation proliferated and evolved in China and Japan. The Jewish practice of meditation also began to evolve, incorporating prayers along with repetitions of teachings. Early Christian meditation can be traced back to the Byzantine Empire. These involved the repetition of a Jesus prayer. Western Christian meditation traces back to the Benedictine monks of the sixth century. Their meditation style differed significantly from that of the Byzantines, Jews, and Buddhists, which usually incorporated a posture and the repetition of a chant or phrase.

The modern form of meditation often referred to as transcendental meditation was developed by Maharishi Mahesh Yogi (1918-2008) in India. He learned the practice from his guru, Brahmananda Saraswati. Maharishi Mahesh Yogi brought this form of meditation to the rest of the world via a series of world tours starting in 1958. Transcendental meditation (TM) involves repeating a sound or mantra and is practiced for 15 to 20 minutes twice a day. Besides

TM, there are many other types of meditation: kundalini, zazen, mindfulness, moving meditations (tai chi and qi gong), self-hypnosis, guided visualizations, etc. Let's take a look at a comparison of these different types of meditation.

Table 12. Different Types of Meditation

Type of Meditation	Origins	Characteristics
Transcendental meditation (TM)	India in 1950's. Brought to West by Maharishi Mahesh Yogi. Origins from Vedic texts (approximately 200 BC).	Generally performed sitting in lotus or half-lotus. Involves the repetition of a mantra.
Kundalini	Like TM, early origins in Hinduism and likely came out of ancient Vedic texts (Vedanta, approximately 200 BC).	Generally performed in lotus or half-lotus. Involves visualizing a stream of energy traveling between cosmos and a central chain of energy centers from the base of the spine to the top of the head.
Mindfulness (vipassana)	Rediscovered by Gotama Buddha more than 2,500 years ago. Common practice in Theravāda Buddhism.	Focuses on being present and letting thoughts run freely without attachment. Often encourages being aware of breathing as well as of other sensations.
Moving meditations (tai chi and qigong)	Tai chi started in the twelfth century in China as a form of martial arts. Qigong is approximately four thousand years old and also started in China.	There are five types of tai chi; each focuses on aspects of health, mediation and martial arts, and is a series of movements and postures. Qigong focuses on the moving of qi, or energy, and is a series of movements and postures.
Guided visualizations	Ancient Hindu texts and early Buddhist writings refer to teaching people to visualize a deity to help bring visualization to fruition. Since time of ancient Greeks up to now, religions have regularly used visualizations for healing or to seek assistance from a divine source.	Listening to audio clips or a live reader who guides the person into a relaxed state in order to achieve specific goals or sometimes just for relaxation.
Self-Hypnosis	Hypnosis was developed by Scottish surgeon James Braid in 1841. He taught his patients self-hypnosis in 1843.	A technique in which a person brings himself or herself into a deep state of relaxation using an inductive method. Once fully relaxed, the person then repeats a phrase that addresses a goal or a phobia.

| Zazen | A Zen Buddhist practice that began in India. It spread to China and eventually to Japan. | Silent meditation practiced in a seated position. Practitioners often sit on a cushion (*zafu*) in lotus position with hands on lap, fingers straight and overlapping, thumbs touching. |

Your Meditation Practice

Which type of meditation is right for me?

First off, you don't have to do a formal meditation like the ones listed above—but if you choose to do so, consider taking a class to teach you the specifics of the practice. Or, you can do your own version of meditation. These are the important components of meditation from the Ekahi Method perspective:

- It should be done daily, preferably twice a day.
- The session should last at least fifteen minutes.
- The goal is to get in touch with your base frequency class by regulating your breathing to your resting breathing rate.
- Remember that your breathing rate (determined in the frequency profile) sets your essential base frequency.

Do I need to sit in lotus position or can I sit in a chair?

If you choose to do your own version of meditation that incorporates the above components, you do not need to sit in any specific position. The main thing is for you to be comfortable. Sitting with a straight back is a good idea as it allows you to breathe fully and expand your lungs and ribcage. You can sit or stand or move with your mindfulness.

How to breathe?

Since your main goal is to bring your breathing rate down to base levels, start slowing it down by breathing in through your nose and out through pursed lips. Once your breathing has slowed to a base level, you can just breathe naturally.

What do I think about or focus on?

Some of the meditations listed above require you to focus either on breathing or on a scene described in a guided meditation. As you can see from the variety of meditation types, there are many different ways to achieve a state of relaxation, which is what you need. Experiment with focusing on different things in your meditation until you find something that works well for you (for example: a flickering candle held in the darkness of your mind). Here are some other suggestions:

- Focus on the beating of your heart by holding a hand over your chest.
- Focus on a serene and relaxing setting.
- Focus on breathing.

Whatever you decide to focus on, keep in mind that it is a tool to help you deepen your relaxation. As thoughts enter your mind, try to let them pass. Do not give your thoughts time or energy. With practice, you will get better at just letting a thought float through you like a passing cloud on a windy day.

Do I need to repeat a mantra?

This is not necessary, but you may find it helpful in increasing your focus for the first few minutes. A mantra is simply a sound, word, or phrase that is used to create a positive outcome or to deepen the meditative state. A common mantra is the word *om*, which you say on each exhalation. Om is an ancient Sanskrit word used in many religions in which meditation is a central component. In the ancient Vedic texts, om is said to be the primordial sound of creation itself.

You can choose a sound or sounds that resonate with you for your mantra. The other type of mantra is a group of words that express something you wish to be manifested within yourself. For example, you might say, "My body is healthy, strong, and free of disease." You can say your mantra silently to yourself, or out loud.

Where should I practice meditation?

I am a big believer of practicing meditation in a variety of locations, such as at work, while sitting outside, or on the bus. It is a good idea to create a space in your home where you feel most comfortable meditating, but in order to really develop your meditation skills, you should practice wherever you can. I like to meditate on long flights or before I go on stage.

What if I can't sit still?

This is a common problem. With practice, sitting still gets easier, but there are also moving meditation such as qigong and tai chi. Some people find deeper meditative experiences in movement. Even walking can be very meditative. The central component to meditation is a focus on present-moment awareness. I have found walking to be very effective meditation if I work on mindfulness and put effort into not letting my mind wander. If you do want to try mindfulness with walking, keep your eyes open!

Optional Tools to Assist with Resetting

The purpose of meditation is to reset to base frequency. It may be hard for you to begin the process of meditation if you are significantly out of balance. We have developed the Ekahi Method base-frequency-resetting scents (body sprays, roll-ons, and candles), scientifically formulated and tested to be effective for each of the five base frequencies. We recommend a few pumps of the body spray prior to meditating. It is also a good idea to put some of the roll-on on your pulse points (neck and wrists). Lighting one of the Ekahi Method soy candles also helps to set the stage for an effective meditation.

We have found that application of the appropriate resetting base frequency spray, roll-on, and/or candle immediately helps one to reset and encourages a mindful state for meditation. It is also a useful tool to use when you cannot meditate (for example, when you are driving). Using the body spray or roll-on will help you start to reset to base frequency.

Visit the Marketplace section of the Ekahi Method website (www.ekahimethod.com) to order these products. Be sure to order the correct item for your base frequency.

Resetting in an Emergency

Sometimes meditation can be useful in an emergency. We all experience anxiety in our lives—it could be before the start of a race, before public speaking, or before a test. Sometimes, this anxiety can develop into a full-blown panic attack. If we don't control the symptoms of elevating anxiety, we could find ourselves in a situation that could be life-threatening. For most people, anxiety is temporary and mild, but for others who experience regular anxiety, it can occasionally manifest as a panic attacks. Symptoms of a panic attack include hyperventilation, excessive sweating, rapid heart rate, and elevated blood pressure. Meditation, if practiced regularly, can be an effective tool to quickly settle those symptoms. It is estimated that over six million Americans suffer from panic attacks. Research has demonstrated that meditation can be an effective tool in managing anxiety and panic attacks (Kabat-Zinn et al., 1992). The more mediation is practiced, the less likely it is that panic attacks will recur. Practicing mindfulness can also be used to slow one's breathing and heart rate. We have also found that the Ekahi Method base-frequency-resetting spray or roll-on can help begin the process of calming and resetting.

Meditation for Finding the Natural Zone

So far we have talked about the importance of meditation for resetting to base frequency. It can also be an effective tool for finding the natural zone. I sometimes find, after work or a presentation, that I am riding too high on my wave. An effective way to come down gently from the crest of the wave toward the natural zone is to sit for twenty minutes and focus on breathing. Meditation can also be used to pull up on the wave if you are stuck in a trough. Sometimes feelings of depression can be ameliorated by focusing internally and not on external matters. Research has shown that meditation can be effective in managing depression; see the research described in table 13.

Table 13. Selected Research on the Effectiveness of Meditation

Reference	Result
(Schneider et al., 2012)	A randomized control trial of over two hundred men and women participated in transcendental meditation and *significantly lowered their risk for cardiovascular disease and lowered their blood pressure*.
(Davidson et al., 2003)	After eight weeks of mindfulness meditation, subjects *produced more antibodies after immunization for influenza vaccine.*
(Luders, Toga, Lepore, & Gaser, 2009)	In people who regularly performed meditation, *the area of the brain which controls emotional responses was more developed.*

(Moss et al., 2012)	After eight weeks of meditation subjects experienced overall *improvement in mood and reduction of anxiety—these correlated with changes in blood flow to the brain.*
(Hölzel et al., 2011)	When sixteen subjects participated in an eight-week mindfulness experiment, MRI showed measurable changes in the brain: There was *increased activity in areas of the brain responsible for learning and memory and emotional response control.*
(Ramel, Goldin, Carmona, & McQuaid, 2004)	The study found that eight weeks of mindfulness meditation were *effective in reducing depression and ruminating thinking.*

Dr. Brett Says

- We have now learned that meditation is an important practice in the Ekahi Method for resetting to base frequency and finding the natural zone on your wave. Meditation is an incredibly subtle, yet powerful tool. The research above shows that this practice not only is helpful for depression and anxiety, but also literally changes brain tissue.

Case Study

A patient came to see me with complaints of chronic pain in her upper shoulders and neck. In addition to the neck pain, my patient complained of difficulty sleeping, weight gain (over thirty pounds in last two years), high blood pressure, and a general feeling of malaise. I asked if she had tried any treatment to alleviate her symptoms. She rattled off a list of practitioners and healers as long as her arm. All of them had provided some temporary relief but nothing lasting.

I completed a frequency profile on her and determined that her base frequency was red but that she clearly had very low energy. I spent over an hour examining my patient until I was ready to provide her with a comprehensive treatment program I was confident would be successful. As I told her this, her eyes widened with anticipation. She asked, "What are you going to do to my neck?" I had almost forgotten that it was her neck and shoulder pain that brought her to see me in the first place!

I explained that her neck and shoulders were not the source of the problem. The pain was a symptom of her having neglected her base frequency for too long. Like many of my patients, she was working in a high-stress job with coworkers of very different frequencies. Her having been in this environment for many years without resetting had caused a chronic health problem. I finally told my patient that the treatment program to address her chronic neck and shoulder pain was *meditation*. Unsurprisingly, she had been expecting something a little more hands-on. I had to remind her that the reason she had this problem was a lack of self-care.

I asked my mediate twice a day, sitting in silence and focusing on breathing. I also recommended a base-frequency-resetting spray. She was to do this for six weeks and then return. I also asked her to stop all other hands-on treatment and focus only on meditation and breathing. She was skeptical as she left my office. As I customarily do, I sent my patient a reminder e-mail along with my report of her findings.

Six weeks later, an emotionally overjoyed woman came through the door, a believer of the importance of regularly resetting to base frequency. It is the most important treatment I prescribe to my patients.

In Summary

- The most important way to reestablish your base frequency is through a form of meditation.
- While there are many different types of meditation, the common goal is to settle the mind.
- Whichever form of meditation you choose, make an effort to consistently practice for at least fifteen minutes every day.
- Research has found many other health benefits to regular mediation practice.
- To assist with resetting, a customized base-frequency-resetting spray, roll-on, and candle can be highly effective.

PART IV

Frequency Tune for Success

CHAPTER 11

What Is Frequency Tuning and Why Should We Do It?

All human beings are interconnected, one with all other elements in creation.
—Henry Reed

Now that you have learned what your own frequency is, how your frequency can be affected by environment and by other people, and how to reset your frequency for health, we are going to learn how to adjust your frequency to match that of another person in order to temporarily improve a work setting, have a job interview, negotiate a deal, or communicate with members of the public. This is known in the Ekahi Method as *frequency tuning*.

As I described previously, people of each of the five frequency classes often have distinct body language. Recall that people in the red base frequency class have closed but relaxed body language. People in green class have a more dominant posture and focus and intensity. People in the violet class tend to appear nervous, anxious, or have very energetic body language. By now you should have experienced how being in the company of somebody with a different frequency than you may cause feelings of slight distress. I also showed you via case studies that when people spend a lot of time with other base frequencies in a work setting without resetting to their own base frequency, chronic disease can result.

What if, instead of being pulled out of base frequency and/or having your wave flattened, there were a way to intentionally adjust your frequency to the same level as another person? Suddenly, a normally draining situation might feel more comfortable—energizing, even. This is frequency tuning. Besides increasing your energy, frequency tuning allows you to create a positive outcome in a relationship with a neighbor, coworker, employee, or even your partner. Let's start with some background on frequency tuning before we look at specific applications.

Dr. Brett Says

- Frequency tuning can be a powerful technique for temporarily improving a situation. When I am in a situation in which I think it might be helpful to improve understanding between myself and another person, I can adjust my base frequency to match theirs. After temporarily using this technique, it's important to reset to base frequency. Remember that one of the ways your base frequency can be moved out of natural frequency is by your matching or tuning into somebody else's base frequency. This should only be done on a temporary basis.

Frequency tuning comes down to matching the frequency of the person you are dealing with. Imagine you are a red frequency class and you are trying to return a damaged appliance to a department store. The employee is a green frequency class. He is making intense eye contact and leaning forward slightly with erect posture. His voice is strong and clear and his thoughts and corresponding words are logically ordered and objective. As a red frequency person, you are now in a challenging situation. You are dealing with somebody who of a higher frequency who tends to be competitive and not want to lose. If you are to have a successful outcome, you must demonstrate to the green employee that you can rise to the challenge. If you were to remain at your base frequency as a red, you will, in all likelihood, be trampled and leave the situation deflated and frustrated.

Important Point

- In this chapter we learn how to use the Ekahi Method to match from the outside, which will then create an internal frequency match. It is important that you do not take the power of these techniques lightly; they are extremely powerful methods. In each of the exercises in this chapter, you will learn how to match things like body language, eye contact, and voice modulation. When you practice these exercises, only experiment with people of the same sex as you. Since matching frequencies can create a very harmonious situation and a highly energetic environment, people of the opposite sex may misinterpret your actions. Also, while you are still learning this skill, you may not be as subtle as you think!

So, how do you frequency tune? The steps are the same for all frequency classes:

1. Match body language.
2. Match eye contact and eye emotion.
3. Match voice rate and pitch.

Let's examine each of the steps individually.

Brett Wade, PhD

1. Matching Body Language

The old saying, "Fake it till you make it," definitely applies here. There is no doubt that we humans are slightly narcissistic. We generally like ourselves and people who are similar to us. Some sources say that up to 85 percent of the information exchanged in a face-to-face conversation is nonverbal. In other words, in conversation we convey most of our meaning through body language and of course, waves.

As we will learn, these skills can be extremely effective in work situations, where we desire a positive outcome while dealing with people in public.

These are kinds of body language that can be matched:

- head or posture: head forward, head in middle position, head back to give appearance of flat neck
- shoulders: slumped forward, held back, or elevated toward ears
- abdomen: soft and protruding, tight and flat, curled backward in a C-shape
- pelvis: shifted to one side, tilted forward to increase curve in small of back, tilted back to flatten low back
- hips: legs wide apart, legs close together, feet turned in, feet turned out. If sitting: legs crossed, legs naturally resting apart, legs held tightly together
- knees: slightly bent, fully straightened, hyperextended (knees bent backward)
- feet: arches flat, arches natural, arches high, weight on forefoot or toes (tiptoe walker)
- limb movement: hand-talking, rocking on feet

The following figures show two of the more easily identifiable extremes of posture. Practice matching the postures in the figures.

Once you can easily move in and out of all the postures, literally matching them from head to toe, it is time to practice for real.

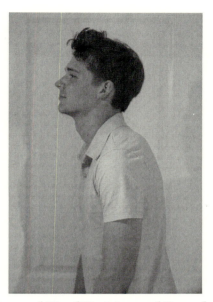

Figure 25. Forward Head Position and Rounded Shoulders

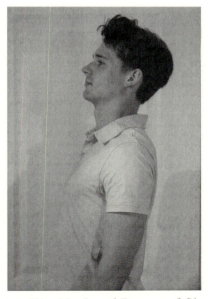

Figure 26. Flat Neck and Retracted Shoulders

An Exercise

Find somebody you don't know who is sitting in a public setting—on a park bench, in a chair at the mall, on the grass outside, etc. Be close enough that you can read their body language accurately, but not so close as to be obvious or disrespectful. A reasonable distance is between twenty and twenty-five feet. Try matching from them from head to toe and notice how it affects the way you see or think about this person. The more alike we are, the more we have affinity with and understanding for other people.

How did you feel when you matched the person? Describe any emotions you experienced:

_____
_____

2. Match Eye Contact and Eye Emotions

Our eyes are the most powerful way we communicate with other people. The way we use our eyes is also a part of our culture. In North America, we are generally taught that eye contact is important because it conveys honesty and interest. However, for some First Nations in North America, maintained eye contact is uncommon (Chiefs, 2008). Likewise, in Japan, eye contact is disrespectful; Japanese children are often taught to look at the teacher's throat instead of his or her eyes. In some Asian, African, and Latin American countries, extended eye contact is considered a challenge or a threat. In some Middle Eastern cultures, intense eye contact between people of the same sex is a sign of respect, but anything more than a fleeting glance between the opposite sexes is frowned upon.

We also convey emotion through our eyes. Think about the eyes of somebody who is surprised, happy, polite, sad, angry, interested, flirtatious, compassionate, concerned, contemplative, contemptuous, pained, or embarrassed. All of these emotions cause distinct changes in the muscle tension around the eyes. Next we will try another exercise, this time matching eye contact and eye emotion with a stranger. But first, let's see how good you are at reading emotions in eyes. Visit the following hyperlink to take a test developed by psychologist Simon Baron-Cohen: http://glennrowe.net/BaronCohen/Faces/EyesTest.aspx

An Exercise

This exercise is to be done with somebody you don't know, but this time in a professional or business setting. It could be done with a server in a restaurant, a clerk in a department store, or a cashier in a supermarket. Please remember: to avoid mistaken intentions, choose somebody of the same sex as you. Once again, subtly match the person's body language (head position, arm position, position of hips and legs). Now matched their degree of eye contact degree and the emotion in their eyes. What do you notice?

How did you feel when you matched this person? Describe any emotions you experienced:
_____
_____

3. Match Voice Rate and Pitch

The speed and pitch of your voice is one of many characteristics unique to yourself; it is a major part of your identity. From the moment they are born, babies can recognize the sound of their parents' voices; they have been listening to these voices for the past several months from inside the womb. In addition, the sound of a mother's voice has been shown to have significant effects on heart rate and brain development (Fifer & Moon, 1994). Even a person with significant brain injury that leaves the brain in a persistent vegetative state can distinguish their of the mother's voice from the voices of strangers (Machado et al., 2007).

First we need to understand how we make noises, sounds, and words at all. The first sound we make as infants is crying. This sound is made simply by taking a big breath in and forcing the air out through the throat. Babies have not yet developed conscious control of the muscles of the larynx, or voice box.

The natural pitch of your voice is determined by genetics. The flexibility of the muscles of the larynx and the overall size of the larynx determine the natural pitch and range of one's voice. The average frequency (or pitch) of the male voice is 85 to 180 Hz and the average frequency of the female voice is 165 to 255 Hz. The extremes of voice frequency range from approximately 80 Hz (a bass voice) to 1,100 Hz (a soprano). To create a higher voice pitch, we contract the muscles surrounding the opening of the larynx to create a smaller opening.

Anatomical aspects of the nose, mouth, and back of the throat take sound from the larynx and allow it bounce around before leaving the mouth. Finally, sound from the larynx is given its unique texture by muscles in the throat and by the size of the opening formed by the mouth. While it is difficult to match someone else's unique voice and not recommended in person as it could be seen as a form of mockery, matching voice pitch is less difficult. If you have ever taken singing lessons or sung in a choir, you know all about pitch matching; this is harmonizing with the notes on played by an organ, piano, or guitar, and then matching the pitch of other people singing.

So, matching pitch is a matter of hearing sound and matching it. People who are really good at this are said to have perfect pitch. Even if you don't have perfect pitch, you can learn to improve your pitch and to match the pitch of other people. You will start by listening to your favorite song and singing along.

An Exercise

In order to hear pitch clearly, it is best to play sound through speakers in a small, enclosed space like a car, shower, or small room. This enables you to receive the benefit of the sound bouncing and staying with you for a longer period of time. After listening to a few bars of music, rewind the song and try singing. The goal is *not* to sound like the singer, but to harmonize, or match the pitch of the song. Practice until you feel harmony. When you match the pitch, you will literally feel a vibration in your head or your body—it is a lovely feeling to be in harmony!

The second part of the exercise is to match voice cadence, or rate of speaking. You have probably noticed that some people speak quickly, others slowly. Find a person in a professional setting (post office, restaurant, dry cleaner, etc.). As you practice matching the pitch of their voice, also practice matching their rate of speech. What do you notice?

How did you feel when you matched this person's pitch and rate of speech? Describe any emotions you experienced:
_____
_____

Other Considerations for General Matching

Personal space: Some cultures and people prefer to be close when they are talking, while others prefer to maintain a greater distance. Be sensitive to personal space when matching.

Physical contact: Be aware that some cultures and people have preferences and sensitivities regarding physical contact in conversation. For example, some people are regular "slappers"—these are the people who, when talking to you, make light slapping contact on your shoulder or forearm. Another excellent chance for matching is handshakes. Shaking another person's hand is an immediate opportunity to match tension and the length of time you maintain the handshake. Keep in mind that some cultures and religions forbid handshakes between men and women.

In Summary

- *Frequency tuning* is a powerful technique to temporarily employ if you need to improve the outcome of a situation.
- Frequency tuning is done by subtly matching the body language, gestures, rate of speech, posture, eye contact, etc., of another person.
- In frequency tuning, you are matching the base frequency of the other person.
- Frequency tuning requires you to move out of your base frequency; as such, it should only be done temporarily. You must reset to your base frequency as soon as possible afterward.

CHAPTER 12

Frequency Tuning for Public Relationships

If you want to find the secrets of the universe, think in terms of energy, frequency, and vibration.
—*Nikola Tesla*

One of the beautiful things about life is the variety of people in it. While being around people of the same frequency may raise my energy, if I only associated with people of my own base frequency, it would be a pretty dull life. I love the opportunity to meet all kinds of people. I enjoy the challenge of trying to match the tone of somebody of the violet frequency class. I know when I can frequency tune to match them, I have a good chance to learn something about that person. Every person has an interesting story, and the closer you are to matching their frequency, the more likely they are to share it with you. I always feel so privileged when I get to learn something personal about another human being. No matter who you are, if you are reading this book, you probably spend time each day surrounded by people who are not of your frequency class.

Of course, you do not have to try to match frequencies with other people. Most of the time, I don't feel the need to adjust my frequency;

I only do so if I think it will improve the outcome of a meeting, when I can tell that if I don't frequency tune, the relationship, meeting, discussion, or transaction will not go well. Often, people are nervous to meet me because they think we are going to find ourselves locked in a frequency matching game. Trust me when I say that I spend most of my time happily in my own frequency.

The following are reasons why matching might be necessary with the public:

- negotiating a deal for a purchase
- disputing a fine or a ticket
- coming to an agreement in a meeting, at work, or with a group of people
- working on a project with a group of people
- your job requiring you to work with the public
- getting work done on your car
- returning an item to a store
- sending back a poorly cooked meal

Important Point

- The goal of frequency tuning is to achieve a positive outcome for both parties.
- Frequency tuning is *never* to be used to manipulate, dominate, or win.

Let's look at some scenarios that relate to the above situations.

Negotiating a Deal for a Purchase

Imagine that you are in a store, planning to purchase a new stove. You have done your homework and know the same stove sells for $200 less at a different store in a nearby town. You can immediately tell that the salesman is of the green frequency class. He describes the stove with active body language and stands erect with his shoulders back and his chest forward. He leans forward slightly and has intense, focused eye contact. He speaks quickly in a middle-range pitch. If you do not have naturally similar body language, you will likely be dominated and in no position to negotiate.

Let's say the old you tries to negotiate with the salesperson. What would the outcome be? I am willing to bet that in most cases, the old you would gain nothing. The salesman would merely flatten your energy, you would not get the deal you want, and you would have to either waste time driving to the other store to save $200 or pay the price this store advertises. Now let's see how frequency tuning changes the outcome.

This time, instead of being dominated by the green salesman, you frequency match. You stand up tall, pull your shoulders back, match the position and movement of the salesman's hands, position your hips similarly to his, and match his eye contact and intensity. Now it is time to use your voice. You go for a pitch match. Of course, if you are a soprano, you are not expected to match his tenor pitch, but rather to find a resonant pitch. Now, what will you say? Using a cadence matching his, you try, "I might be interested in this stove if it were $200 less." The salesman increases his body energy, maybe crossing his arms, and says, "I have no room to move on this price." What do you do now?

You cross your arms, increase your energy, and say, "Listen, your competitor is selling this exact same stove for $200 less, and while I really like this store, and I would like to see my money stay in town, it would be irresponsible for me to pay more than I should." The salesman now raises his pitch slightly and starts to speak a little more quickly. You also notice that his face is slightly redder and he is starting to lose his eye contact. At this point, you are close to making a deal.

The salesman tries one more time and says, "Look, I can only do so much, and you are comparing prices in a different town. I will speak with my manager and see what I can do." Congratulations, you are already further along than you likely have ever been! Now, here is the critical part. You must keep your composure and be prepared to continue to match when he returns. You must ask yourself, "What am I willing to accept?" If the salesman comes back with only a slightly better deal, like $50 off the ticketed price, you have some more work to do. If, however, he comes back with a deal that meets you halfway, you might decide that it is fair and that it covers the gas and time you would lose driving to the next town.

Remember, above all else, that the Ekahi Method of negotiation is not about dominating, but coming up with an agreement that satisfies both parties. If you decide to use the Ekahi Method for purposes of domination or manipulation with the intention of winning the interaction, then this method is not for you—you have missed the point. The point is to have both parties feel they have won something. This is the spirit of the Ekahi Method for negotiations.

Dealing with a Customer Who Has a complaint

Let's say for example, you have a job that requires you to deal with the public. Perhaps you are a server in a restaurant, a manager in a company, a checkout clerk in a grocery store, a physician or nurse who works with patients, or a teacher. It is safe to say that almost every vocation deals with the public in some aspect. On a daily basis, you will likely deal with people with whom you would normally never choose to associate—but in order to do your job, you must effectively deal with all kinds of people.

The techniques are the same, regardless of vocation. Whether you are a teacher trying to connect with a student, a health care worker trying to relate to a patient, or an employee trying to work with a customer, your job is to deliver the highest level of service to the client, customer, or student. In order for both you and the customer to feel that you have had a successful experience, you should use the Ekahi Method to frequency tune.

Often, employees must deal with customers who are dissatisfied with a product or service. The Golden Rule in business is, "The customer is always right." I have a slightly different take on the rule. I think the rule should be, "The customer must be heard." A customer with a complaint or concern may be the most important customer you ever have; for every customer who complains, there are another twenty-six who are also dissatisfied but not saying anything. By actually hearing the customer, you have a chance to make your business better. Making the business better makes your job better.

How do you effectively hear somebody? You must match their frequency. In the previous chapter we went through ways of frequency tuning by matching body language, body movements, voice, and eye contact. If you can do this with each customer, you will make them feel that they can actually share with you; then you may hear more valuable feedback. Too often, when a customer has a complaint, employees immediately become defensive or too quickly try to solve the problem and get the client out the door. Now let's imagine you are a server and a customer has a complaint.

You have just brought a bowl of clam chowder, a sandwich, and a glass of chardonnay to your customer and asked her customer if she needs anything else. She says no so you leave to wait on other tables. Later, you return to this customer's table and ask her what she thinks of the meal. Much to your surprise and horror, she tells you that this is the worst clam chowder she has ever tasted, the sandwich has soggy bread, and the chardonnay was served warm in a dirty glass. Your immediate reaction is to follow protocol and tell her you will get her a new order—but is that all there is to the problem?

In a well-run restaurant, or any business for that matter, you should view every customer as critical to the survival of your business. There is no shame in finding out the specifics of the customer's concerns. Instead of immediately rushing off and giving the customer more or less the same version of what she just ordered, it is more valuable to find out specifically what did not meet her expectations. Start with frequency tuning. Once you have matched the customer's body language, eye contact, and voice, you tell her how much you value her feedback and ask her specifically what was it about the soup that was not satisfactory (temperature, flavor, consistency). You listen to her answers and write it down. Ask the same questions regarding the sandwich—besides the bread, is there anything else that she would like to see improved? About the wine: Were just the temperature of the wine and the cleanliness of the glass inadequate, or was the wine list itself inadequate? You are engage the customer, but do not interrogate her.

Your customer's answers show genuine respect and interest. At this point, you do everything you can to correct the meal and drink, possibly suggesting another dish. In addition, all of this must be communicated to the manager, who also visits the table and tells the customer that he has heard her concerns (he restates them to make sure he heard them correctly) and appreciates them. Finally, to make sure this customer gives the restaurant another try, she is offered a gift certificate for a free meal for two. This is how a customer is heard using the Ekahi Method. This example can be used for any situation in which a customer or client has a complaint or concern.

Making Recommendations to a Client

For this example, let's imagine a health care provider who is seeing a client for chronic health issues such as obesity and high blood pressure. She must make recommendations about diet and lifestyle to this client. A successful outcome in this case would be for the client to feel that he has been heard and that somebody cared, and for him to follow the recommended program and achieve its goals.

This is one of the most common scenarios in health care. The health care practitioner might be a doctor, a nurse, a physical therapist, a naturopathic physician, or a personal trainer. Having worked in health care for many years, I can tell you not only what has worked, but also, what does not work for making recommendations. Before I started to frequency tune, I had a success rate (meaning that the client successfully achieved the recommendation goals) of around 30 percent. It took me a long time to realize that while I had the best intentions, I was recommending programs to patients without really hearing them. Once I started to frequency tune, my outcomes changed. Now I estimate over 90 percent of my clients achieve the goals that we co-develop.

When a patient comes to see me, I make sure to listen carefully, not only to their concerns but also to their fears, desires, and what they see as barriers to achieving their goals. For patients to feel that they can share the most vulnerable aspects of their personalities, they need to feel matched. By subtly adjusting my body language, voice, and eye contact, I frequency tune so I can hear clients perfectly and paraphrase their responses. In this state, clients are likely to tell me the reasons they may not be able to do their daily exercises.

Frequency Tuning for Crisis Intervention

You may never have had to deal with a hostile situation, but there is a good chance that you will someday. You might be threatened verbally, physically, or emotionally, or you might have to intervene to settle a situation between other people down.

In either case, the person who angry or hostile needs to have their energy brought *way* down—and quickly. The fastest and most effective way to do this to raise your intensity in an effort to intensity match and build rapport. Ideally you want your intensity to be just below theirs; if their intensity is at 9 out of 10, you want to be at 8.5.

The reason your energy should stay just below theirs is that if it were higher, it could inflame the situation. You don't want your energy any lower because then you would risk either seeming patronizing or being completely bowled over by their intensity.

Important Point

- Do not intentionally put yourself in a volatile situation just to practice this technique. It takes a significant investment of time and training to become proficient in frequency tuning. The above recommendations are only to be used in emergency situations.

In Summary

- Frequency tuning can be effective in negotiations. The technique is not about dominating, but about working to find resonance and the best outcome.
- Frequency tuning can be used for many application in dealing with the public, from handling complaints to helping clients make decisions.
- Frequency tuning can be used for crisis intervention, but only in emergencies. Do not seek to test your new skills in a volatile situation if it is not necessary.

CHAPTER 13

Frequency Tuning for Personal Relationships

Invisible threads are the strongest ties.
—*Friedrich Nietzsche*

This section teaches frequency tuning to improve your current relationship, or to find a new relationship. We have learned that people of different base frequency classes are unique in the way they express their energy emotionally, physically, socially, and mentally. We have learned some techniques for adjusting or tuning our frequencies to temporarily improve a relationship with another person or group. This chapter is about using the Ekahi Method for our most intimate relationships; it explores how to maintain and improve relationships, and how to forge new ones.

Whether you are in a committed, long-term relationship or want to find an individual and forge a new relationship, it is important to consider the effect of your base frequency class on your partner and on yourself. Frequency tuning in a relationship may sound like a lot of work. You might be thinking, "I just want to be myself!" You are right, you definitely should be yourself, especially with your partner.

But learning to frequency tune with your partner will deepen and improve your relationship. It can allow you to ride a wave together.

You already know what your base frequency is. Perhaps you have also discovered your partner's base frequency. In this chapter, I will address the following questions:

- What if my partner and I are different base frequencies? Will the relationship work?
- How do I frequency tune with my partner?
- How much frequency tuning should I do in a relationship?
- Should a potential partner be the same base frequency color as me, or different?
- Do I want friends from all base frequency classes, or should I aim to find friends of my base frequency color (or close to it)?

What if my partner and I are different base frequencies?

This is very common and not a reason to be concerned. Many successful relationships exist between couples of different base frequencies, even red and violet. As long as each person in the relationship honors their own base frequency and regularly resets, there is no reason even the frequency opposites can't have a wonderfully fulfilling relationship.

Dr. Brett Says

- Two people of any base frequency classes can have a successful relationship as long as they both understand the importance of respecting their own base frequency, resetting to base frequency, and tuning their base frequency as needed.

Case Study

Recently, a close friend of mine was talking to me about whether I thought he and his girlfriend were a good match of energy for each other. I had met my friend's girlfriend on several occasions and thought they both appeared to have a lot in common. Both my friend and his girlfriend had completed the frequency profile many months ago, so I knew that he was red and she was yellow. Being this close on the spectrum, they had similar energies but he was concerned that she didn't energize him and make him feel vital. I reminded my friend that the frequency profile provides a guideline by which couples can note where their natural base frequencies are and how they may interact with each other. I told my friend that he couldn't expect his girlfriend to be responsible for his energy—he had to take responsibility for finding his own natural zone on his own wave, and he should respect his girlfriend's journey in finding that same position on her wave.

I asked him if he felt his relationship had changed in terms of energy, and when that change might have occurred. He said that for the last couple of months, he had been feeling low in energy. He had stopped exercising regularly and had not been eating as healthily. He implied that because he was often sitting on the couch with his girlfriend instead, his lack of vitality was her fault. I reminded him again that he alone was responsible for finding his natural zone and that he could not blame his girlfriend for how he was feeling. I asked him to try for six weeks to recommit to regular exercise and a sensible diet. Sure enough, six weeks later he was once again feeling vital and he and his girlfriend were back to doing things together.

Brett Wade, PhD

How do I frequency tune with my partner?

Now we know that a relationship can theoretically succeed between any two base frequencies, what is the point of frequency tuning? We have seen that frequency matching, when necessary, can be a powerful way to create resonance and increase energy. Let's imagine that you are yellow and your partner is blue. Your partner is going through a difficult period of his life and is struggling to raise his own energy to the natural zone. If you match his frequency, you can not only demonstrate that you care and are listening, but also possibly resonate and naturally raise his energy. While this might be a temporary measure—he could revert back to his low spot on the wave—a few sessions of working to match his frequency might help bring him back up.

If you are in a long-term relationship, the next time your partner is low on the wave, try this:

- Find a time when you can dedicate at least thirty minutes to listening.
- Ask your partner to sit across from you or, preferably, sit at a slight angle to each other.
- In a very subtle way, match one aspect of your partner's body language—head position, shoulders, legs, hand or arm placement, eye contact, etc.
- Ask open-ended questions and genuinely listen. For example: "I've noticed you seem a bit down lately. Is there anything you would like to talk about?" Be patient with your partner and give them time. If they do not want to talk, ask if you can just hang out with them.
- Try listening to some music you know they enjoy.

If you try this technique a few times, I am confident you will find success.

Won't my partner think I am mimicking him/her?

I get asked this question a lot. Let me assure you that even if they know about frequency tuning in the Ekahi Method, your partner will appreciate your efforts and concern. Remember, this is not about trying to fool or deceive your partner, and it is definitely not about manipulating them, either. It is about tuning into your partner to understand and support them, and to develop a better connection. When we learn to ice skate, or snowboard, or dance, we are awkward at first, but we become more graceful and comfortable with practice. Likewise, once you get better at frequency tuning, it will be no more obvious when you do it than spontaneously looking your partner right and in the eye and saying, "I love you."

Here is a caveat: If your intention is to deceive or manipulate, it is extremely likely that your partner will perceive this and indeed feel that you are mocking them.

A recent article on the website of UK newspaper *The Daily Mail* referenced research (Bates, 2013) that showed:

- A couple's breathing patterns and heart rates synchronize when they are in close proximity to each other. Interestingly, this effect was not observed in paired-up strangers.
- Women seem more able to naturally synchronize their heart rates with their partners' heart rates.

These findings are consistent with the foundations of the Ekahi Method. Synchronizing with another person is a process that is not only emotional, but physiological as well.

How much frequency tuning should I do in a relationship?

There is no simple formula to calculate the answer to this question. During stressful times for your partner, more frequency tuning may be required. As you get better at the technique, you will be able to sense when you need to frequency tune—just make sure you reset to your own base frequency.

Remember, it is fine for couples to spend time apart; time apart helps you to restore your natural rhythms. If you are in a situation in which you must spend a lot of time together (going on a trip together, working on a project together), you will have to frequency tune more often in order to keep things going smoothly. Be very aware of whether or not you are in a good spot on the wave yourself. Make sure to reset.

Dr. Brett Says

- Do not attempt to frequency tune with your partner if you have not taken the time to reset to your own base frequency. You will only be successful in frequency tuning if you are coming from a restored place yourself.

Case Study

Two years ago a new patient with a sports-related injury came to see me. Ashleigh, twenty-eight, was a recreational long-distance runner. Her physical assessment and treatment were relatively straightforward, but I sensed an overwhelming sense sadness from her. I asked specific questions to determine whether she was out of balance with her base frequency. A frequency profile showed her to be yellow.

She spoke quietly but freely, stating that she was a girl who had always "done everything right"; she had been a good student through school and university and was now a successful healthcare worker. She worked hard and did whatever she could to make everyone else happy, but she was not feeling happy herself. She had thought that by this time in her life she would have been married, sharing a happy life with a loving partner. More than anything, that was what she wanted.

She had taken up running at the age of eighteen and ran 5 km a day. I knew that, because she was a yellow, this was a good form of exercise for her; running is rhythmic and solitary. Running made her feel centered and grounded and it had always restored her. Up until now she had never had an injury.

She had recently joined a running group and became enamored with a man in it. He was training for a marathon and asked her if she would be interested in doing the same. Because she wanted to get closer to him, she was very excited to say yes to this proposition. She pushed herself harder and harder to keep up with him, but was never very impressed by or pleased with her. He never wanted to spend time with her beyond training, and he did not seem at all curious about her life. He talked a lot about himself, talked a lot to others, and at times even referred to her as his girlfriend, but she still felt invisible. Even though she was spending a lot of time with him and they seemed to be in an exclusive relationship, she was confused, unhappy, and now physically hurt as well.

She lamented, "I'm doing everything that he seems to expect of me, but he does not seem to be in love with me. It doesn't matter what I do." I could see that she had been physically pushing herself so hard that she developed injuries. More importantly, though, she was pushing herself far out of her base frequency, and as a result, she was frustrated and suffering emotionally.

I prescribed Ashleigh some basic stretches, but also, I asked her to meditate daily to get in touch with and reset to her base frequency. I suggested that she tell this man that she would love to run 5 km a day with him (her running natural zone) and then meet up with him later.

When I saw her a few weeks later, she was glowing and happy. She said the man had noticed her radiance and opened up to say to her, "You are the only woman I have dated who makes me feel happy." By honoring her own base frequency and nourishing herself, she became happier and healthier.

I was not surprised when a frequency profile revealed the man's base frequency to be blue. This is an example of how people of different frequencies can be drawn to each other—but it is not good if one of them is bending himself or herself out of shape. By honoring her own base frequency, Ashleigh became happier. An unexpected outcome was that she became more attractive to Mr. Blue. It could have gone the other way; he could have lost interest in her because he had gotten used to her being a certain way already. However, he found the real Ashleigh to be more attractive and, interestingly, to make him feel better about himself.

She told me she was feeling so good that she didn't mind only being friends with this man, but because he was suddenly so caring toward her, she was compelled to explore the relationship further.

What if I frequency tune all the time with my partner, yet my partner never makes any effort to meet my energy wave?

This can be an exhausting and frustrating situation, much like Ashleigh's was. If you continually come out of your own frequency but your partner never does, then it is up to you to decide whether the relationship is working for you. It is not uncommon in this situation to feel like your partner does not understand you, no matter what you do.

However, I have seen many couples in which one partner is very naturally skilled at frequency tuning but the other does not reciprocate. Despite this, the frequency tuning partner is happy to continually do so in order to maintain a functional relationship.

Dr. Brett Says

- Remember that when two waves of similar frequencies come together, they summate, and there is resonance. Resonance is very lively and exciting. It feels great—creativity and sparks in the relationship can fly! Resonance can also be fatiguing. You don't want to be riding the crest of the wave all of the time. It's important to come down off the crest so you can ready yourself for the ride back up again.

Once you have found the natural zone in your relationship, you will notice:

- You naturally listen to each other attentively.
- You want to converse and share with each other.
- You are sensitive to the moods and feelings of your partner.
- You recognize your partner's body language and know how to read it accurately.

- You are more likely to use words like "we" and "our".
- You respect and encourage your partner to be happy and autonomous.

When you are riding either too high or too low on the wave, you will notice:

- You listen poorly to each other and have frequent misunderstandings.
- You want distance from each other and do not feel like sharing thoughts or feelings.
- Your partner's feelings may irritate you.
- You are out of touch with each other's body language.
- You are more likely to use words like "I" and "mine".
- Your lives feel parallel to each other, not together.

Finding True Love and a Lifelong Partner

The most important thing to keep in mind in using the Ekahi Method to find a partner is that if you are in touch with your own base frequency, you will automatically attract people who are good partners for you.

Think about it this way: We have probably all been in social situations in which we worked hard to impress others, trying to do and say what we thought they would like. If you have to go significantly out of your base frequency to have fun with people, you are not likely to find someone with whom you can easily sustain a long-term relationship.

Dr. Brett Says

- You will be at your most attractive to a potential long-term partner when you are in tune with who you are and your base frequency; then you will find someone who resonates with you. So tune in to yourself and see what if feels like to be with people who are attracted to what you are. We are all products of a society that tends to prescribe how we should be and what we should do. You may think that attractiveness is achieved by being extroverted, bubbly, confident, chatty, successful, fashionable, thin, fit, or sporty. But I am telling you that you will be most attractive, most happy, and most likely to find a wonderful partner by being yourself! Tune into your own base frequency, respect it, and resonate with those who feed your frequency.

Should a potential partner be the same base frequency color as me, or different?

If you are a yellow, for instance, you may decide it would be advantageous to be in a relationship with somebody who is either also a yellow or at least close in frequency, like a red. First of all, somebody of the same frequency will tend to raise your energy. This can be useful if you are somebody who has difficulty overcoming entropy. In other words, if you are naturally prone to low energy and riding low on your wave, being with somebody of the same frequency may help you overcome your entropic nature.

If, on the other hand, you are naturally prone to riding high on the crest of the wave (this can happen for any color), then being with somebody of the same base frequency could be quite destabilizing and fatiguing. The trick is figuring out a potential partner's color. On a first date, people generally put out their maximum energy to impress the other person. If you are trying to determine a color frequency on a first date, good luck! You might be able to determine whether a person is red or violet, but you will likely have some difficulty picking up the other three colors.

Here are some good questions to ask on a date to help determine someone's color frequency:

- Are you a morning person or a night hawk?
- What kind of activities do you prefer to do?
- Do you like being around lots of people, or do you prefer limited and organized social interaction?
- Do you like a household with an "our house is your house" philosophy, where friends and family are free to come and go, or do you prefer your home to be a quiet sanctuary?
- When you travel, do you go with the flow by observing and steeping in the culture, or do you like a predictable schedule packed with lots of events?
- What kinds of places/environments do you prefer?

These questions will start guiding your intuition in determining your date's frequency color.

As you get to know the person, observe their behavior to help you figure out their base frequency. Are they talkative with everyone, moving easily from one person to the next, or are they quieter with a preference to speak to one person at a time for long periods? Do they move quickly or slowly?

Do I want friends from all base frequency classes, or should I aim to find friends of my base frequency color (or close to it)?

Because we spend limited time with friends, it can be extremely fulfilling to have friends of all base frequency colors. I am certainly drawn to people of all base frequencies and find their friendship fulfilling and expanding in different ways. You may find it a lot of fun to spend time with someone who is quite different from your base frequency. You can play sports, work on a project, or just socialize together—just make such to reset as necessary.

I would venture to guess that your closest friends resonate easily with your frequency, and vice versa. You *get* each other. I would also venture to say that you have friends who are great fun, or intellectually stimulating, or good sports partners, but spending a few hours or a weekend with them makes you think, "Wow, I am exhausted!" and "I love being with that person, but can't spend too much time with them." It is likely these people are not resonant with your base frequency. It can be very fulfilling to be able to appreciate and spend time with people of all frequencies. If you are looking for a long-term partner, however, you will likely feel more nourished, more like yourself, and more understood if you are with someone who resonates easily with you. They may not be the exact same base frequency as you, but they are able to respect and understand you and to feed your frequency.

It is also important to make sure you resonate with any friend with whom you are planning to share an apartment or a house, or to travel for a long period.

In Summary

- You do not have to find somebody of the same frequency to have a successful relationship, but you do need to respect the importance of regularly resetting to base frequency.
- Respecting your own base frequency is the key to finding a successful relationship.
- Frequency tuning can be used in a long-term relationship to fully understand and help a partner who is stuck at the bottom of a wave or teetering at the top.
- When two partners are together riding the natural zones of their respective waves, they experience a magical moment of clarity, respect, and sensitivity.

- There are ways to recognize base frequency in another person (chapter 6).
- Only you are responsible for affecting your position on your wave; you cannot expect your partner to consistently bring you to your natural zone.

CHAPTER 14

Decision Making and Developing Intuition

I believe in intuitions and inspirations ... I sometimes feel that I am right. I do not know that I am.
—*Albert Einstein*

Have you ever been faced with a big decision like a major career change or a big, expensive purchase, and been worried about making the right choice? Big decisions can instill severe anxiety about the consequences of making the wrong choice. How can we use the Ekahi Method to improve decision making and reach the best outcome? The one focus of the Ekahi Method is to be in tune with your *base frequency* so that you are familiar with your normal state of physiology. The sensation of being out of your natural frequency is a stressful one.

We have learned that certain environments and people can dramatically decrease our own energy. What about our own thoughts? Can what we think about affect our frequency and amplitude? There has been much research devoted to this subject. In the 1930s, Walter Cannon, a physiologist at Harvard Medical School, studied the fight-or-flight response, a physiological reaction that occurs in the body in very stressful situations, causing changes in blood flow, blood pressure, heart rate, and sweat levels.

This stress response can be triggered by both real dangers from which one must fight or flee, and imagined dangers. Your body doesn't know the difference between your fear that the results of a medical test will come back positive and your fear on actually receiving positive results. Imagine yourself in a stressful situation: What happens to your heart rate, your breathing rate, your muscle tension? If the imaginary event makes you anxious enough, your body could respond with the same level of stress you would have if you suddenly found yourself surrounded by sharks while swimming in the ocean.

Something to try

- Close your eyes and imagine a stressful situation. It could be something real or made-up.
- What do you feel when you visualize or remember this scene?
- Does your heart rate go up? Does your breathing rate quicken? Do you develop tension in parts of your body? Do your hands become cold?

If you experience any of these symptoms, that means your body is in the fight-or-flight response. This can be help ensure your survival in an emergency, but you will not, most of the time, be in an actually life-threatening situation. By developing a better relationship with your stress response, you can consciously ask yourself whether the stress response is helpful or an exaggerated response to a non-life-threatening situation. Learning to control this stress response will allow you to achieve better outcomes.

A classic example of a non-life-threatening situation that triggers an exaggerated stress response is public speaking. Most people find the thought of standing in front of a group and speaking incredibly stressful. Typical stress responses in this case are increase in voice pitch, decrease in voice volume, increased heart rate and blood pressure, increased muscle tension, and sweating. Why do people find public speaking so frightening? There is no real need to fight or flee. If you could control your stress response, you might be able to enjoy the experience and make it enjoyable for those listening to you.

The first step to learning to control your stress response is to be aware of it. Once you are aware that a non-life-threatening situation is triggering extreme physiological responses, acknowledge this fact and tell yourself, "No harm will come to me in this situation. I am calm and relaxed and I will enjoy this experience."

Dr. Brett Says

- Our thoughts can trigger strong feelings and physiological reactions that can be scary. A thought alone can make you sweat or make your heart race. Fortunately, our thoughts can also make us smile and feel happy. Even now, many years later, thinking about the birth of my children immediately makes me smile. When we consider the best choice we can make, we are looking for a subtle feeling of contentment. The signs will not be overt; you will not suddenly grin widely or start jumping for joy, but feel a little vibration of happiness.

Decision Making

Any decision usually involves a multitude of choices. Rarely is there just one right or wrong decision. However, usually one decision will lead to the best possible outcome. How do you know which one that is? The answer has to do with paying attention to your body's stress response. Even the most mundane decisions and choices will trigger a physiological response in you.

Think about a lie detector test. Did you know that a lie detector works by measuring the person's stress response? The subject is hooked up to numerous sensors that measure things like heart rate, blood pressure, breathing rate, sweating in the hands, and muscle tension. When the subject truthfully answers questions, there will be no observable stress response. But if the subject answers untruthfully, the lie creates a stress response, and the polygraph will detect a physiological change in the subject.

It is, of course, possible to gauge your own stress response without a lie detector.

Something to Try

- The next time you are at a restaurant you have never tried before, carefully look over the menu. You are faced with a variety of choices of things to eat. How do you decide which dish you will enjoy the most and which dish your body requires?
- Look at the menu slowly and read each menu choice to yourself. After reading a choice, wait for a response. You will notice that some items cause a slight change in your physiology when you read them. Any feelings of stress (increase in muscle tension, upset stomach, sweating, and increased heart rate) indicate an incorrect choice. If you have no physiological response, the choice could be neutral or a possible right choice. Continue this process with each menu item.
- The correct choice causes feeling of contentment and happiness in you. This emotion is subtle; therefore, it takes practice to be able to sense correct choice.

Feeling for Best Decision

As I mentioned in the previous experiment, it is easier to sense the physiological stress response that suggests an incorrect decision than it is to sense a best decision. The best decision will not induce any stress response—in fact, it brings forth subtle feelings of contentment and happiness. What does this feel like?

Contentment and happiness are the opposite of stress. When you are happy and content, you are relaxed; your heart rate and breathing rate are low, and you are in your base frequency class somewhere around the natural zone.

Therefore, the best decision brings you closest to feeling like you are in your natural zone. You will feel contentment and peace. Your choice will make you feel at home in your frequency. This method of gauging physiological response can be used for literally every decision that you make. Some people are naturally good at it; good things seem to flow to them easily. Some regard these people as lucky; in actuality, they are simply intuitive with decision making.

What Is Intuition?

The word intuition comes from the Latin word *intueri*, which means to look inside or to contemplate. A modern definition of the word is: to acquire knowledge without inference and/or the use of reason. Many people think of intuition as the province of alternative healers and psychics, but it is an important part of the evolution of modern-day psychology.

In the early 1900s, Carl Jung described people who sense their world predominantly with intuition as *intuitive type*. Intuition is simply knowing something without reason. Before our brains developed to be able to reason logically, we survived by intuition and instinct. Our early ancestors must have had heightened intuitive senses. They could likely sense if they were being stalked by a predator—they had to be able to do so in order to survive.

It is not unreasonable to believe that some people are just better at sensing and knowing the invisible world. We live in a society in which only that which can be tested, verified, and seen to be true is respected. Some might say that we need intuition less and less to survive now. However, I believe the opposite to be true. A poorly developed sense of intuition might result in your blithely ambling down a dark alleyway, unaware of danger lurking around the corner, or unaware of a stalking cougar while you're on a hike. In her book *The Intuitive Way*, Penney Peirce says that intuition is a vibration experienced in our primitive, reptilian brain, and she describes the sensations of intuition as they rise from the reptilian brain through to a midbrain level, and then finally to a conscious level.

Pierce describes the midbrain intuitive sensations of smelling, touching, tasting, seeing, and hearing as abstract representations of messages bubbling up from that reptilian sensation of vibration. She says the final stage of intuition is applying our neocortex brain to ascribe labels and language to what we feel. If we are in tune with our intuition, we should be able to detect subtle sensations from the slightest vibration through the midbrain and then to describe the experience.

Dr. Brett Says

- Intuition is developing the ability to detect subtle changes that are, essentially, resonance or constructive interference. We have learned in previous chapters that the resonance of being around people of similar base frequency may increase our own energy. Intuition is the same, except those same subtle feelings can be induced merely from a thought. Think about the first time you felt you were in love: That feeling likely resonates with you and raises your energy slightly. Developing best choice is asking yourself if a decision is best for you and looking for that subtle feeling. With practice, you will get better at it.

Making the best decision is all about paying attention to the subtle physiological changes in your body. Intuition is the formal process of looking within to get in touch with those physiological changes. When you are about to make a decision, look within and see if you can feel a vibration, listen for that little voice, or see the symbols that tell you which decision is best for you.

Developing Intuition

Did you know that we have muscles to spread our toes apart individually and to move our ears? Chances are you can't willfully do either of those things, though. Over the course of human evolution, we stopped using these muscles. We started wearing shoes, and we no longer needed to position our ears to listen for danger; thus, we lost the ability to use these muscles. The same goes for intuition. We used to be much more intuitive, but as our world became safer, we let go of the need for intuition. The good news is that just as we can retrain the muscles of our toes and ears, we can retrain our lost functions and abilities of intuition.

Now, more than ever, people need to develop their sense of intuition. Now that there is so much less face-to-face communication between people, we need to develop our intuition for the decision making that protects us and helps us thrive in this world. I think that intuition is the difference between the person who seems stuck in a rut with bad luck always following them and the person who seems to be lucky in life. The life we live and paths we choose are the result of a continuous stream of choices. From the moment we wake up in the morning we choose—when to get out of bed, which clothes to wear, what to eat, how to feel, which route to drive, what to think about, what to listen to, etc. We face millions of choices each day.

You may not think that you are choosing your mood or thoughts, but in fact you are always choosing. Many choices are unconscious; this is a useful trick of the brain. It would be exhausting to have to consciously think about every each decision in our lives. The brain converts a decisions to the unconscious mind as soon as we integrated that choice into a pattern, or routine. But what if that pattern is a bad one? Could it be possible that some of your unconscious choices are actually bad for you? We could have many patterns that are not the best, but we have stopped checking in with ourselves and we have cease to be intuitive. If you feel unlucky or that you're going through a period of tough times, it may be time to start asking yourself, from the moment you get out of bed, whether there are better choices to make.

It may seem like a silly exercise to stand in front of the open refrigerator and ask yourself, "Do I want my usual breakfast, or would my body prefer some other choice, like a grapefruit?" Believe it or not, though, the correct answer lies within you as a slight vibration, as Peirce calls it. Practice this with as many decisions as you can to see if you can feel it.

Once you relearn intuition, you can better your life and the lives of those around you.

Something to Try

The next time you are about to make a seemingly mundane decision such as whether to a blue blouse or a red blouse, ask the question this way: "Is the blue blouse the best choice for me?" Then wait about five to ten seconds for a feeling. Next ask, "Is the red blouse the best choice for me?" Once again, wait five to ten seconds. The feeling will be very subtle, as there is not likely to be a lot of emotion riding on the decision.

Try this technique with most of your day-to-day choices for at least four weeks. With practice, you just might notice your luck start to change!

Case Study

> A family member of mine recently came to see me in tears. Her life was a shambles. I had only known a little about her troubled life; as she poured her heart out to me, I was taken aback. Since she was a child, trouble had seemed to find her. She had had terrible relationships and even worse break-ups, she had been in car accidents, she had had legal trouble, she had been fired from many jobs, she had numerous health problems—the list went on and on.
>
> The hardest thing was knowing that she was a really good person who seemed to be unlucky. You might know somebody like this yourself. For years I had offered her advice that never seemed to help—in fact, it had soured our relationship for many years. When she came to see me this time, she had lost it all. She had been kicked out of the place she was living, lost her job, and was spiraling into a bad state.
>
> I immediately tried to settle her down, but she just kept saying, "Why am I so unlucky in life?" With her in that state, I could not offer anything more than a shoulder to cry on, but I offered to show her something that could help

in the morning. She agreed to try anything. We both slept poorly that night. In the morning, I set to work. I asked her to write down all the choices she made in a typical day. She looked at me quizzically. I gave her a piece of paper and her to work do the task. Ten minutes later, I returned to check her progress. To my astonishment, she had not been able write down a single choice.

She started to cry, feeling as though she had somehow failed me. I reassured her that this was a clear starting point for turning her life around. I said to her, "Please write down that you chose to participate in this exercise." She said, "I didn't really have a choice." I reminded her that at no time had I told her she *had* to do anything. She agreed and wrote it down. Then I helped her write things like "Choose to press snooze or get up with alarm," "Choose buzzer or radio station when setting the alarm," "Choose which side of the bed to get out of," "Choose which socks to wear," "Choose a pair of pants," "Choose which sock to put on first"—you get the idea.

With my help, she wrote down a hundred choices she made before noon on a typical day. We could easily have come up with over a thousand. What is the point of this exercise? First, to see the multitude of choices you face in every moment, and two, to start developing your intuition for finding the best choice. We had fun and some good laughs while making the list.

The next task was to start developing her intuition. We went to her suitcase and I asked her to pull out two shirts. I had her ask herself, "Which shirt do I prefer?" She asked the question for each shirt and waited for a feeling of resonance and contentment. It took several tries, but eventually she started to have fun with the game. I asked her to try this exercise over the rest of the day for at least a hundred different choices. She stayed with me for a week and we kept practicing. Then she received a call that would test her intuition. It was a friend from work offering her a place to stay and a part-time job. She experienced the feeling of best choice and moved out to her new life. Although she does not now win the lottery regularly or hobnob with the rich and famous, she does seem happy and more successful with finding best choice.

An Exercise

How many choices do you make in a day? Using the table below, make a list of them, with one alternative per choice. Start from when you wake up until noon. For example, when you wake up, what do you do first: shower before having breakfast, or eat breakfast before showering? Once you have finished, practice asking yourself the question of best choice for each one. Can you feel anything? Your ability will improve with practice. If nothing else, you will realize that you do always have a choice! Write your decision in the Decisions column.

Table 14. Your Choices in a Day

Time	Choices	Decision
When I wake up	*a) shower before having breakfast, b) eat breakfast before showering*	*Shower first*
When I wake up		
Noon		

In Summary

- Thoughts have feelings associated with them.
- A negative or worrisome thought may raise your blood pressure, heart rate, and breathing rate.
- A happy thought makes you smile, puts you at ease, makes you less tense, and raises your energy.
- A right choice creates feelings that raise our energy, resonate with us, and make us feel like we are in the natural zone.
- We must start to develop the ability to sense this subtle feeling whenever we make a choice.
- Intuition is merely the ability to recognize the feelings which thoughts or choices induce.
- Unlucky people usually don't realize that they have choices and don't know how to feel for best choice.
- With practice, you will get better at feeling for best choice.

PART V

Nourish Your Body with Resonant Frequencies

CHAPTER 15

Resonance with Food

Let food be thy medicine.
—Hippocrates

We have learned that intuition can be used to find best choices, which resonate with use and make us energized and happy. In this section, we are going to learn to resonate with food, music and sound, exercise, and our own environment. We will learn the basics about the importance of having these things in our lives and make sure to understand that when it comes to resonance, one person's pleasure is another person's pain.

By now, you should be practicing resetting to *base frequency* for at least thirty minutes a day. You should be spending time getting in touch with your natural rhythms every day. There are many things that can disrupt our own base frequency, like people of different frequencies and man-made sources of unnatural frequencies and intensities. What about the foods we eat—can they affect our energy? The answer is yes, indeed!

This book is *not* a diet prescription. Recall that the Ekahi Method is about one thing: the frequency of waves. Now, can food have a frequency? Yes, as a matter of fact, it does. It may surprise you to learn that there is debate about whether fruits and vegetables are alive or dead when you eat them. Once a vegetable or a fruit is picked, it begins to die. A human who has suffered a severe stroke may have begun the process of death, but with proper treatment and the right environment, that process can be delayed. The same is true for an apple, carrot, or broccoli. When you pick the fruit or vegetable, you cut it from its life source of water and sugar; from then on, it is slowly dying.

How, then, can dying, decaying food have a frequency? Back to the human who has suffered a stroke: He may be in the process of dying, but his body continues to carry out the physiological processes of digestion, energy production, waste production, fluid movement, etc. Fruits and vegetables are somewhat similar. After they have been picked, they lose the connections that were feeding them with sugar and water. Many fruits are picked before they are ripe and are allowed to ripen in a grocery store or at your home. This is a slow process of decay. It is often said that eating fruits and vegetables is good for us. Many people accept that information without considering why and how.

Enzymes

Eating fruits and vegetables as soon as possible after they have been picked ensures that you are eating foods that are as close as possible to being living. Live foods are high in natural enzymes, which are proteins that are vital to thousands of different chemical reactions in the body. Enzymes function as catalysts, speeding up chemical reactions and ensuring specific desired end products. Enzymes are involved in reactions like the breaking down of sugars, proteins, and fats in our digestive tract, as well as in complex reactions like the synthesis of DNA. Our bodies produce nearly all the enzymes we need. While there is debate about whether eating foods high in natural enzymes is helpful or not, it makes sense that eating foods high in enzymes assists digestion.

Since enzymes are mainly proteins, they are likely to be damaged by cooking. Therefore, if there are health benefits to eating foods high in natural enzymes, then it is important to eat them raw. Another controversial subject is so-called "enzyme deficiency." Recently, articles and supplements have shown up on the web claiming that if people are deficient in enzymes, they may benefit from enzyme supplementation. A review of scientific literature shows that enzyme deficiency is a relatively rare genetic condition. That said, a deficiency of lactase (the enzyme required to break down animal milk products) is relatively common; many people are lactose intolerant. However, most people are unlikely to be deficient in enzymes.

Vitamins and Minerals

So what are the real benefits of eating fruits and vegetables? There are extremely important health benefits to eating foods that contain vitamins, minerals, fiber, and antioxidants (vitamins A, C, and E, flavonoids, carotenoids, phenolic acids). Fruits and vegetables supply our bodies with important minerals such as calcium, iron, sodium, potassium, magnesium, zinc, and copper. Our bodies use these minerals for vital functions like building bone, transmitting nerve signals, regulating heart rate and blood pressure, and making blood. Minerals also have an important role linking with enzymes to carry out important functions such as digestion. Fruits and vegetables are excellent sources of vitamins. Vitamins are cofactors, which means they are necessary like important cogs in machinery. Vitamins can act as free-radical scavengers, help build tissue like bone, protect parts of the brain and spinal cord, and help make certain hormones.

Dr. Brett Says

- The daily news and information about what to eat and what not to eat can be dizzying and often contradict what we once thought was right. One thing you can always count on to be good practice is eating food of the highest frequencies: fresh fruit and vegetables. The more colorful and natural your food is, the more it will resonate with you and nourish your base frequency. When in doubt, eat more fruits and vegetables.

Antioxidants

Foods high in antioxidants are excellent free-radical scavengers. Remember that while our bodies produce free radicals naturally, certain envrionmental toxins can increase their numbers. A diet high in antioxidants can help neutralize the effects of excess free radicals. The foods that contain the highest levels of antioxidants per serving are red beans, kidney beans, pinto beans, wild blueberries, cranberries, blackberries, prunes, and raspberries. Make sure that you get some of these in your diet every day. It is recommended for you to select a variety of colors of fruits and vegetables each day. Different colors represent different concentrations of antioxidants, vitamins, and minerals. In addition, fruits and vegetables are an excellent source of fiber, which is good for colon health.

Proteins

Still, you could not subsist on fruits and vegetables alone, even with all their health benefits. Your body requires foods which contain fats and amino acids. Amino acids are the building blocks of protein. Proteins, as we have learned, can form enzymes, but proteins also form our DNA and RNA, which contain the genetic codes for building and replacing all the cells and tissues in our body. Most of the twenty kinds of amino acids there are can be synthesized within the body, but nine of them are considered *essential*, which means that they must be obtained through food sources.

Some foods are said to be *complete proteins* because they contain all of the essential amino acids in the necessary proportions. Examples of such foods are meat, eggs, fish, and dairy products. Typically, plant sources of protein are missing one or more amino acids, or else they are not present in the correct proportions. If you choose a fully vegetarian diet, you can easily remedy this problem by combining the proteins beans and nuts in your diet.

Fats

Fats are another important nutrient in our diets. Our brain and spinal cord are approximately 60 percent fat, so it stands to reason that we need fats in our diet. Fats are also necessary for the absorption of vitamins A, D, E, and K. Fats are made up of fatty acids and glycerol molecules. While dietary fat used to be considered bad, we now realized that it is the type of fat that we need to be concerned about. While they have some health benefits, saturated fats—particularly from animal sources such as beef—are correlated with cardiovascular disease. We now know that trans fats, which are man-made, are also associated with increased risk for heart disease. Healthy sources of dietary fat are generally unsaturated (monounsaturated or polyunsaturated), such as the fat from nuts, seeds, fish, olive oil, and avocados.

So in order to keep our energy at normal levels within our frequency, we must eat a healthy diet with adequate levels of vitamins, minerals, antioxidants, essential amino acids, and good sources of fat. In addition to eating healthily, intake of fluids is also vital. Since the body is approximately 60 percent water, we can conclude that water is vital to our survival. Water is essential for regulating body heat, pH levels, electrolyte levels, and blood fluidity, and providing a medium for metabolic processes. We need to take in between one and three liters of water a day. Some of this water can come from fruits and vegetables and drinks like tea and coffee. The color of your urine indicates whether you are taking in the right amount. Urine should be a light-straw color. The following figure (figure 27) is a good guideline for the recommended ratios of different foods.

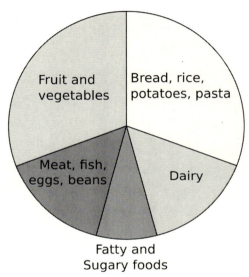

Figure 27. Healthy Eating Plate
By Lionfish0 (Own work) [CC-BY-SA-3.0 (http://creativecommons.org/licenses/by-sa/3.0)], via Wikimedia Commons

Alcohol and Caffeine

Alcohol is neither recommended nor excluded from the Ekahi Method. Alcohol should be consumed in moderation. Note that it does lower energy within base frequency as it is a depressant. In other words, alcohol is a wave reducer. Caffeine is a natural stimulant found in many plants such as tea leaves and coffee beans. Caffeine, like alcohol, has been shown to have health benefits when taken in moderation, but also like alcohol, it can cause problems when taken in excess. Caffeine is a wave amplifier.

Dietary Supplements

With a few exceptions, most research suggests that supplements have little positive effect on health. Generally, they do not have negative health effects, but they may be costing you a lot of money. If one eats a diet rich in colorful fruits and vegetables and follows the above recommendations on proteins and fats, then supplements are unnecessary. Some people do need to take supplements such as iron or vitamin D for medical reasons. It is wise to ask your physician about whether supplements are right for you; your physician's advice should be respected.

Vitamin D is one supplement which seems to be very important for some segments of the population. Vitamin D is a powerful antioxidant. It is only produced in the body when you are exposed to sunlight. so you can increase your vitamin D levels through diet. Table 15 is taken from a study on the efficacy of vitamin D in preventing cardiovascular disease (Lee, O'Keefe, Bell, Hensrud, & Holick, 2008). Oily fish is an excellent source of vitamin D. Most milk sold in North America is fortified with vitamin D. Recent research suggests that people living in northern latitudes or who have limited exposure to sunlight should supplement with approximate 600 IU of vitamin D daily (Glerup et al., 2000). A joint study in 2010 by the US Institute of Medicine and Health Canada came up with the same recommendation of 600 IU for people aged nine to seventy (*Dietary Reference Intakes for Calcium and Vitamin D*, 2011).

Table 15. Excellent Sources of Vitamin D

Food	IU Per Serving
Cod liver oil, 1 tablespoon	1,360
Wild-caught salmon, 3 oz	600-1,000
Farmed salmon, 3 oz	100-250
Mackerel, cooked, 3 oz	345

Tuna fish, canned in oil, 3 oz	200
Sardines (with bones), canned in oil, drained, 1 oz	250
Milk, nonfat, reduced fat, and whole, vitamin-D-fortified, 1 cup	98

From: (Lee, et al., 2008)

Since vitamin D is a powerful antioxidant and can act as a modulator of the immune system, many studies show that vitamin D is useful in the treatment and possibly prevention of some diseases (table 16.)

Table 16. Diseases for Which Vitamin D Has Been Shown To Be Helpful

Disease	Reference
Multiple sclerosis	(Ascherio, Munger, & Simon, 2010; Correale, Ysrraelit, & Gaitán, 2009; Weinstock-Guttman et al., 2012)
Rheumatoid arthritis	(Cutolo, Otsa, Uprus, Paolino, & Seriolo, 2007)
Crohn's disease	(Harries et al., 1985)
Parkinson's disease	(vinh quôc Luong & Thi Hoàng Nguyên, 2012)
Cancer (some types)	(Garland et al., 2006)
Cardiovascular disease (diabetes, high blood pressure, enlarged ventricle, coronary heart disease)	(Zittermann, 2006)

Melatonin

Melatonin is a powerful antioxidant. It has a superb ability to neutralize excessive levels of free radicals. Melatonin is naturally synthesized in the pineal gland of the brain through the conversion of the neurotransmitter serotonin. Melatonin production and release are very much affected by light exposure on our retinas. Bright daylight will stop the release of melatonin and stimulate its production in the pineal gland. A dark environment will stimulate the release of melatonin (usually at night). There is more information about melatonin in chapter 19.

Supplementing with melatonin is a good idea for people who do not receive exposure to bright light in the daytime and/or who have too much light in their rooms at night.

Omega 3 Oils

These are essential fatty acids found in fish oils and some plant oils. You must consume them as your body can't produce them. Research has shown that the consumption of these oils is beneficial for reducing the risks of coronary heart disease (Hu Fb & et al., 2002), rheumatoid arthritis (Geusens, Wouters, Nijs, Jiang, & Dequeker, 1994), Alzheimer's disease (Chiu et al., 2008), and depression (Fontani et al., 2005). These oils seem to work by reducing the body's inflammatory reaction.

Using the Ekahi Method to Find the Best Foods for You

Now that we have covered the basic recommendations, it is time to apply the Ekahi Method to them. Have you ever noticed that sometimes you don't crave your favorite food? If you regularly drink coffee, have you ever noticed that some mornings you just don't want it or find that it doesn't taste the same as usual? You need to start remembering to use your intuition. Your body is very intelligent; it knows exactly what it needs. Unfortunately, we are incredibly good at ignoring our bodies. We treat the body like an insensitive lump that must be beaten into submission. Your body is masterful at trying to get you to eat certain foods or drink more water, but all too often, we are wrapped up in some new diet or program so we deny are bodies, or we feed them something we *think* we want. We let marketers tell us that we need that hamburger or that diet soda. Your body is too smart for that. It is time to put down that supersized soda and listen carefully to what your body is asking for.

Here's how to start:

- Begin by deciding to eat only fresh fruits and vegetables of a variety of colors and healthy proteins and fats every day.
- Decide to have three to five meals a day. Consciously ask your body with each piece of food if it will prefer the food or not. Do this as you hold the food or look at the ingredients of a meal.
- An example: For lunch, you have the choice of pasta with marinara sauce or an egg salad sandwich. When you ask yourself which you would prefer, look at the pasta and then look at the eggs. Take note of the feelings within your body. A subtle sensation will guide you to the best choice. It may seem awkward at first, but stick with it and you will get better at remembering what it is like to have intuition.
- In chapter 14 you practiced developing intuition with food by looking at food items on a menu and feeling for a subtle feeling of vibration. This is the same process.

This is the style of eating promoted by the Ekahi Method, and it is called *intuitive eating*. In the 2012 book *Intuitive Eating* by Evelyn Tribole and Elyse Resch, the authors explain that one of the principles of intuitive eating is learning to "feel your fullness," or in other words, know when you are full. They suggest that you "observe the signs that show that you're comfortably full" (Tribole & Resch, 2012). If you take your time and pause during the process of eating, you will have a chance to experience the sensations of hunger and satiety.

Dr. Brett Says

- Intuition with eating is the same practice as feeling for resonance or wave amplification in the presence of other people. If a food is good for your base frequency, you will feel it on a visceral level. Consciously ask yourself if a food is good for you and your body will provide its answer by way of a subtle wave that will indicate either resonance or that the food is a wave killer. With practice, this subtle wave becomes much easier to detect. Be patient and know that your body will not lie to you.

Food Sensitivities

Over the past several years, many patients of mine have reported food or additive sensitivities. Some sensitivities are to dairy, nuts, MSG, molds, sulfites, and wheat (gluten). It should be noted that food sensitivities are much more common than food allergies. A person has a food allergy when their body actually develops an immune reaction (producing specific antibodies) to a certain food. A food allergy is a more severe and acute reaction than a sensitivity. For example, somebody with a peanut allergy could, just by coming in close contact with nuts, end up in an emergency situation with their throat closing up, making them unable to breathe.

Food sensitivities are quite common. The body's response after consuming a food or additive it is sensitive to is usually delayed. For example, somebody might notice the day after consuming gluten that they have irritated joints in their hands. Or somebody might notice they have a slight rash hours after eating food with MSG in it. Sulfite sensitivities may cause a headache. Most food sensitivity reactions are mild, but cause a person to avoid consuming that food or additive. While there are tests that can supposedly determine food sensitivities, the most reliable test may just be trusting in your body. If a food doesn't feel right for you or gives you a rash, then why eat it?

Brett Wade, PhD

An Exercise

Use your intuition to learn what foods your body does not want. Look for the subtle vibration as you ask yourself whether a food is good for your body or not. Write down your findings.

By using intuition, I have found the following foods to be wave reducers:

_____
_____
_____
_____

By using the intuition, I have found the following foods to be wave amplifiers (I felt resonance):

_____
_____
_____
_____

Case Study

I recently had a patient suffering rheumatoid arthritis (RA). RA is an autoimmune disease in which the body attacks its own collagen. Collagen is the base substance for all connective tissues like cartilage and is the most ubiquitous protein in the body. When your body mounts an attack on your own collagen, your joints, muscles, organs, ligaments, tendons, and bones can all be affected. Since RA is an inflammatory condition, anything that increases inflammation in the body exacerbates the condition, worsening symptoms such as pain, swelling, weakness, fatigue, and malaise. Food sensitivities and food allergies can certainly make the condition worse in this way.

When my patient came to see me, she was in an inflamed state, meaning her RA symptoms had cycled to a point of exacerbated symptoms. As part of my usual evaluation, I had her complete a frequency profile and I proceeded to ask about her lifestyle (diet, exercise, stress, electrosmog in her environment, etc.). I also evaluated the range of motion of all her affected joints, her muscle strength, her flexibility, her nervous system evaluation, and her posture.

I concluded that the patient was a violet frequency class. As such, she had interrupted sleep patterns and low hunger and she was prone to anxiety and fatigue. I found out that she was vegetarian who abstained from alcohol and coffee. She consumed most of her calories from wheat. I thought it might be worth her trying a wheat-free diet as many people have a sensitivity to gluten, one of the main proteins in wheat. I recommended substituting pasta with quinoa and amaranth, as these ancient grains are not normally associated with sensitivities. I also recommended she use essential oils for meditation.

Six weeks later, my patient's symptoms had dramatically improved. In fact, she told me that she had noticed improvement within three days of changing her diet.

The Ekahi Method asks you to listen to your body in order to determine your best diet; it does not prescribe any particular diet or exercise regime. You should determine diet for yourself by using and testing your intuition and feeling for the vibration that tells you that you which foods are wave reducers and which wave amplifiers.

In Summary

- Eat mainly vegetables and fruits that are raw and of a variety of colors (half your daily plate).
- Eat grains from a variety of sources (a quarter of your plate).
- Eat lean/healthy protein daily (a quarter of your plate).
- Eat foods high in antioxidants.
- Drink water regularly throughout the day.
- Limit caffeine and alcohol consumption.
- Be intuitive about the right food for you and knowing when you are full.
- Take note of which foods and drinks might be wave reducers and which wave amplifiers.
- The aim of eating is to bring you into your natural zone.

CHAPTER 16

Resonance with Music, Sounds, and Words

Music is an agreeable harmony for the honor of God and the permissible delights of the soul.
—Johann Sebastian Bach

Are you interested in country music? How about top forty? What about classical or my personal favorite, jazz? Within your favorite kind of music you probably have favorite musicians. I particularly like the music of Stan Getz, Miles Davis, Thelonius Monk, and John Coltrane. For each of these artists, there are certain pieces of music I really like.

What does music say about you? The type of music you like generally represents your frequency class. While your musical tastes, much like your taste buds, change with age, once you reach your midtwenties, your preferred frequency of music remains fairly constant. You might go from being a fan of top forty to liking classical or jazz music, but the essential frequency or timing of the music you like does not really change very much.

Brett Wade, PhD

The Frequency of Music

Music is a series of notes played at a certain rate. Music has certain characteristics that are very much related to waves and the Ekahi Method. Music can be defined by pitch, which is the frequency of a note's sound wave. For example, the pitch of A4 (the A note just above middle C on the piano) has a frequency of 440 Hz. Every note has a unique frequency or pitch.

Music is also characterized by tempo, which is how quickly or slowly it music progresses. The tempo of slow music played at a walking pace is *andante*. *Lento moderato* is moderately slow and *allegro* is a fast-paced tempo. Finally, for our purposes, music can also be defined by amplitude, or how loud the piece of music is. There are other, more subjective characteristics which define music, such as timbre, melody, and rhythm. In the Ekahi Method, we will focus primarily on the pitch and tempo of music and how they can affect your own base frequency and amplitude.

Constructive interference is a term used in physics and wave theory which describes the increase in a wave's amplitude after two waves of similar frequency combine. Have you noticed that your musical preference varies or fluctuates with your moods? People naturally play music that matches their mood. We can think of mood as both the amplitude, or energy, and the frequency of the wave. We have seen that things and people of different frequency classes can have the effect of altering your own frequency. Sometimes, when you are sad, you may find yourself attracted to music which matches your mood, that is, your frequency and your amplitude.

Music can raise your mood to bring you back to base frequency, or irritate you and decrease your amplitude by causing destructive interference. While it may not be possible to draw definitive conclusions about the correlation of your frequency class with music frequency, your personal attraction to certain frequencies of music without a doubt affects mood and physiology. Music can make us cry, laugh, and dance. It can cause us to relax or to get excited. If you enjoy running for exercise, it is quite likely that you do not play ballads when you run, but music with a faster tempo. Music not only affects your mood but it can change your perceptions of the world. A recent study has shown that when people listen to happy music they generally see the world as a happy place and when they listen to sad music, they are more likely to see the world as a sad place (Jacob Jolij, 2011).

Dr. Brett Says

- We don't often think about the resonance of our favorite music. I believe the music you love resonates with your base frequency. We can use music to elevate our mood (wave amplifier) and to bring us down (wave reducer). Both uses of music can be highly effective for finding our natural zone.

Why do teenagers tend to listen to music with quick tempos and high amplitudes? In part, it is because adolescence is a time of rapid development of certain parts of the brain and of overall active frequency. Also, loud music (high amplitude) can allow teens a way of expressing extreme emotions in a safe manner. Anger, rage, and frustration—not atypical emotions in a teenager—fit well with loud, quick- tempo rock or punk.

This is a trick I of mine to help me use music to elevate my mood: First, I play music that matches my current state. This part is quite easy. Then, gradually, over four or five songs, I increase the tempo of the songs I choose until I am listening to music that I normally listen to when I am functioning at my base frequency.

Brett Wade, PhD

I took the time to analyze the key signatures of my top ten favorite songs, and I have found that my favorite songs are in the key of E minor or A minor. If you do not have a background in music theory and do not know the chords of your favorite songs, you can simply find this information by doing an internet search; you will likely find that somebody has transcribed it for guitar or piano (any instrument is fine).

It is quite possible that your favorite music is written in a range of keys. If you do have a favorite key or keys, it might suggest that your attraction to the music has to do with its rhythm. Regardless, the important point here is that music can have a powerful effect, so it is an effective tool for adjusting mood if you need to raise your energy. Some recent research (Nayak, Wheeler, Shiflett, & Agostinelli, 2000; Pacchetti et al., 2000) showed that music can helpful as therapy in the treatment of neurological conditions such as Parkinson's disease and strokes.

Case Study

> In 2012, a, seven-year-old girl in England went to sleep in her mom's bed. The mother noticed the girl was breathing erratically in her sleep. She examined the girl and found her cold and unresponsive, although her eyes were half open. The little girl was rushed to hospital where she was found to have suffered a massive brain aneurysm. She had slipped into a coma and suffered several strokes over the next two days. The family was called in to say their final goodbyes. While the mother kissed her daughter, the little girl's favorite song began to play on the radio. It was a song they had used to sing together. The mother began to softly sing the song and suddenly, the little girl started to smile. The astonished nursing staff told the mother to keep singing. Days later, the little girl was not only still alive, but up and walking around.

Dr. Galina Mindlin, author of *Your Playlist Can Change Your Life*, also references this amazing story. She says, it is possible to activate certain areas in a brain with certain frequencies that are deeply ingrained in the individual since so many frequencies are determined by genetics. "While we are growing and going through different stages of development, those frequencies are changing—yet the most powerful of these can survive, especially those frequencies pronounced in connection with associative memory."

An Exercise

Write down five songs or pieces of music which are wave amplifiers for you and five songs which are wave reducers. The next time you feel out of your natural zone, use these songs to elevate or diminish your energy.

Five songs that are wave amplifiers for me:
_____
_____
_____
_____
_____

Five songs which are wave reducers for me:
_____
_____
_____
_____
_____

Brett Wade, PhD

Binaural Beats

Binaural beats are a perceptive phenomenon in which two notes of only slightly different frequencies are played simultaneously and the resultant sound seems to pulsate. They were first discovered in 1839 by a German inventor named H.W. Dove. The initial discovery by Dove did not garner much attention until it was revitalized by Gerald Oster when in 1973 he published a paper (Oster, 1973) in Scientific American called "Auditory Beats in the Brain." Oster suggested that the binaural beats could be useful in neurological research. Since that time, studies have shown that when some people are exposed to binaural beats, effects such as: decreasing anxiety, decreasing blood pressure, and brainwave entrainment can occur.

Some people have suggested that the so called "Mozart effect" may be due to the apparent use of binaural beats in his music. Whether this is true or not is of debate but it is noteworthy that Albert Einstein was well-known for listening to Mozart to facilitate creativity (Miller, 2006).

The word binaural literally means having or relating to *two ears*. Binaural beats are frequencies which, when combined, create a separate frequency similar to those of brainwaves. For example, by combining a frequency of 500 Hz and another of 490 Hz, you get a resultant wave of 10 Hz. Recall that brainwaves are divided into the following categories:

- (0-4 Hz) Delta waves have the lowest frequency but highest amplitude. They are generated in deepest meditation and dreamless sleep. In addition, certain frequencies within the delta range trigger the release of a growth hormone beneficial for healing and regeneration.
- (4-7 Hz) Theta waves are associated with sleep and deep relaxation.
- (8-13 Hz) Alpha waves occur when we are relaxed and calm.

- (13-38 Hz) Beta waves occur when we are actively thinking and problem-solving.
- (30-100 Hz) Gamma waves occur during complex coordinated activities of the brain. Tibetan monks seem particularly skilled at reaching higher frequencies.

Research (Will & Berg, 2007) shows that auditory sounds can actually entrain the brain to a specific frequency. In 2007, researchers found that even a sound like a drum beat can synchronize brainwaves. A wave of 10 Hz would be suitable for entraining our brainwaves into a calm and relaxed state (alpha waves). Producing a binaural wave that of approximately 5 Hz could entrain deep relaxation and prepare us for sleep (theta waves). Binaural beats require two separate frequencies to enter your ears and then mix to affect your brainwaves, so the use of headphones is required for full effect. In a recent study (Padmanabhan, Hildreth, & Laws, 2005) Binaural beats were found to be successful at lowering pre-surgery anxiety in patients when compared with an audio group (no binaural beats) and a control.

Binaural beats can be used as an adjunct to your daily meditation. If you are having difficulty reaching a relaxed state, binaural beats could help you. Binaural beats can also be useful if you are attempting to entrain to a specific brainwave. If, for example, you want to increase your brain's problem-solving abilities, you might want to entrain your brain with binaural beats during meditation to reach beta brainwaves.

Meditating with binaural beats can provide these benefits:

- decreased anxiety and stress
- increased confidence
- enhanced creativity
- improved ability to concentrate and focus
- better sleep

Of course, there are other, more simple methods of generating a frequency in order to stimulate your brainwaves; repeating a mantra during meditation can achieve this too. A mantra is a word, phrase, or sound that is repeated to assist in deepening the meditation. I often repeat the word *om* in meditation to assist me in reaching a deep and focused state. The word om originated in the ancient Sanskrit language and is a mantra that has been used for thousands of years. It is an important word in Hinduism, Buddhism, and Jainism. While it may have slightly different translations and spellings across cultures, it is generally believed to be a sacred word referring to God or the supreme creator. Hindus believe that as creation began, the divine, all-encompassing consciousness manifested as the sound *om*.

Besides its sacred meaning and origins, I like the sound of this word because when I repeat it, it slows my breathing down, and also, it sounds to me like a binaural delta wave. I find using this mantra leads to clear and calming meditations. Of course, you don't have to use the word om. Devout practitioners of transcendental meditation are encouraged to discover their own mantras and then keep them secret. If you do choose to meditate with a mantra, make it one that feels right to you. You will know it is right because just saying the word makes you resonate.

The Power of Words

Words can convey significant energy that is either positive or negative or neutral. Much of the energy of words is based on your cultural experience with them. The lyrics of a song can move us, but it can be difficult to determine whether that feeling isn't actually caused by the music's melody, rhythm, or key. Words by themselves can, without a doubt, be powerful. Think about the power of profanities. Whether you approve of their use or not, they are some of the most powerful and, some would argue, important words in our vocabulary. Again, culture affects our experience and emotion regarding words. I have a French-Canadian friend whose first language is French, although she is fluent in English as well. Like many French-Canadians, she was raised a Catholic. While she doesn't go to church on Sundays anymore, for her, the most profane words are related to the Catholic Church and considered taboo to say. She will easily roll four-letter words off her tongue as a normal part of her daily conversation, but she would never curse with words that are considered *sacré* (sacred, so they should not be said) like the word *tabarnac* (tabernacle).

There are, of course, many racist, sexist, and xenophobic slurs that I would never use because of the extreme negative energy they carry. On a more subtle level, even words like dumb, stupid, fat, dork, geek, spaz, idiot, loser, lazy, and ugly can be very negative and cause significant reactions within us. Sadly, by the time most of us reach adulthood, we have heard and said at least a few of these words. Even if you have been called any of these words for decades, they might now cause strong physiological reactions in you such as increased sweating, heart rate, blood pressure, and muscle tension. This shows you the power of words.

Negative words affect your energy in a very real, negative way. Self-talk can be very destructive. How many times have you called yourself stupid, dumb, fat, dork, or idiot? How many times have you thought to yourself, "I will never achieve this," or "I will never get that job," or "I will never lose this weight"? Don't make the mistake of thinking that negative words don't have the same effect if you say them to yourself silently—they do!

Brett Wade, PhD

Dr. Brett Says

- When we learned about intuition, we learned that thoughts can create sensations and symptoms in the body. A thought can literally change your physiology. A word can have the same effect. Words can be wave reducers or wave amplifiers. If you use negative self-talk, you could be preventing yourself from reaching your natural zone.

In her book, *Your Body Believes Every Word You Say: The Language of the Body/Mind Connection*, Barbara Levine describes overcoming a brain tumor. She says that her diagnosis was an opportunity to take a look at all the things she had done to co-create this disease and to look for any and all methods to assist her in her recovery. Amongst other things, she began to consider the effect that years of self-doubt, fear, and negative thinking had had on her health. She analyzed her negative self-talk and tried to consciously reprogram herself to use positive words and speak about herself in healthy and positive ways. She had surgery to remove the tumor attributes her state of remission to the change in how she communicates with herself.

Now you must consider whether your own words are negatively affecting you. You cannot control what other people say about you, but you most certainly can control what you say about yourself. When you catch yourself starting to engage in negative self-talk, correct yourself immediately and change the words to positive ones. If you walk past a mirror, look at yourself, and start to say, "Oh my God, I am so fat! I have got to lose 20 pounds!" you must immediately stop yourself and instead say something like, "I appreciate the effort I am putting into losing weight and I am starting to look and feel better." While this may seem awkward and maybe even disingenuous, you must try to work at it. The more you say positive thing, the more you believe them, and the more your body starts to believe, as well.

In Summary

- Nourish your base frequency using sound or music.
- Listen to music that increases your energy whenever you need it.
- If you need to lower your energy, try soothing music.
- Consider listening to binaural beats to assist with your meditation.
- Consider using a mantra with your daily meditation
- Remember that words have energy and while you cannot control what people say about you, you can control what you say and think about yourself.
- Words and some music can be wave reducers or wave amplifiers.

CHAPTER 17

Resonance with Exercise

> *If we could give every individual the right amount of nourishment and exercise, not too little and not too much, we would have found the safest way to health.*
> —*Hippocrates*

We have discussed how food, music, sounds, and words can nourish your base frequency. Now we will discuss the important subject of exercise, which can also nourish your *base frequency*. For some of you, the word exercise has negative connotations, for others it conjures up images of ultramarathons, and for others still, exercise is gardening or climbing a flight of stairs to your apartment. There is no one correct definition of exercise. The Ekahi Method teaches you to find both the exercise that is right for you and the right time to do it.

Let's begin with some important statistics about exercise. Research has shown that exercise increases life expectancy. The authors of a recent study (Reimers, Knapp, & Reimers, 2012) of this very subject stated, "Physical activity reduces many major mortality risk factors including arterial hypertension, diabetes mellitus type 2, dyslipidemia, coronary heart disease, stroke, and cancer. All-cause mortality is decreased by about 30 percent to 35 percent in physically active as compared to inactive subjects."

Brett Wade, PhD

While there is great debate in the scientific community about how much exercise is needed (time per exercise session and number of times per week) and how intense it should be (percentage of maximum heart rate) to achieve the benefits of increased life expectancy, there is no question that doing even a little exercise on daily basis is helpful. A recent study by Steven Moore of the US National Cancer Institute and his coauthors (Moore et al., 2012) found that as few as seventy-five minutes of physical activity per week can add nearly two years to your life. That means that doing just over ten minutes each day of physical activity that makes you sweat and breathe hard enough that you could not easily have a conversation will have significant health effects. The researchers also found that brisk walking for just over an hour each day was associated with adding an additional four and a half years to your life. Regardless of your opinion about exercise, if you want to live longer and healthier, exercise is vital. The Center for Disease Control and Prevention lists these benefits of exercise ("Physical Activity and Health," 2011):

- weight control
- reduced risk of cardiovascular disease
- reduced risk of type 2 diabetes and metabolic syndrome
- reduced risk of some cancers
- strengthened bones and muscles
- improved mental health and mood
- for older adults, improved ability to do daily activities and prevent falls
- increased chances of living longer

We have already seen how exercise can prevent disease and help us live longer. Now let's look at some of its positive effects on our mental health and mood. One benefit of exercise is that it helps us sleep better. One study showed that walking as few as six blocks a day helped people sleep better and reduced episodes of nightmares (Sherrill, Kotchou, & Quan, 1998). Over forty million Americans suffer from some form of anxiety disorder. A study in 2010 (Saeed, Antonacci, & Bloch, 2010) examined the effectiveness of not only traditional exercise, but also adding yoga, tai chi, and qigong to traditional exercise routines such as walking. The authors found that traditional forms of exercise, when combined with yoga, are highly effective at reducing anxiety and are comparable to medical treatments such as medication and cognitive behavioral therapy. High-energy exercise and regular aerobic exercise (three to five days per week) proved to reduce depression symptoms.

Another study which analyzed all available research on the topic of exercise and depression (Craft & Perna, 2004) found that exercising even for twenty minutes a day, three days per week, had a significant effect on reducing the symptoms of depression. While there are numerous theories as to how exercise reduces depression and anxiety, the most accepted one is that exercise triggers the release of hormones and neurotransmitters (chemicals that stimulate other nerves) which are a natural sedative and have a feel-good effect.

So how does exercise relate to the Ekahi Method and your frequency class? Well, exercise moves your body, and movement always occurs in a wave. It is important for the exercise that you do to be in resonance with your frequency. Recall from chapter 9 that your base frequency is most energetic at certain times of the day. You must try to exercise when you are close to 4 or 5 on the energy scale that you drew in chapter 9.

Most people perform better at physical activity when they are warm. Coordination tends to be better because warmth makes muscles more responsive and less likely to tear. Your basal temperature is likely to be highest when you are at the peak of your energy.

Some people seem able to pop out of bed and start exercising immediately. If you are someone who feels most active in the morning, you are likely a green, blue, or violet base frequency.

If you feel most active in the afternoon or evening, then that is when you should exercise. Understandably, you will not always be able to schedule your exercise according to your base frequency rhythm, but when you do have the ability to choose when to work out, you will get the most benefit and enjoyment if the exercise time matches your circadian rhythm. Most red frequency class people prefer *not* to exercise first thing in the morning, but in the late morning or in the evening.

Taking Your Temperature

Over the course of a day, take your oral temperature every three hours from the time you get up until the time you go to bed. Record the values here. It is normal for your body temperature to have daily fluctuations between about 1.5 degrees. Once you discover when your body is at its warmest in your circadian cycle, try exercising at that time.

- 6:00 a.m.: _____ degrees Celsius/Fahrenheit
- 9:00 a.m.: _____ degrees Celsius/Fahrenheit
- 12:00 p.m.: _____ degrees Celsius/Fahrenheit
- 1:00 p.m.: _____ degrees Celsius/Fahrenheit
- 3:00 p.m.: _____ degrees Celsius/Fahrenheit
- 6:00 p.m.: _____ degrees Celsius/Fahrenheit
- 9:00 p.m.: _____ degrees Celsius/Fahrenheit

Types of Exercise to Nourish Your Frequency Class

To summarize, we now know that doing exercise is important not only for obvious indicators of health but also to nourish our base frequency—this will keep us healthy on all physical, mental, and spiritual levels. Now let's look at the types of exercise that are best for each class.

Table 17. Typical Preferred Exercises for Each Base Frequency

Base Frequency Class	Typical Exercise Preferences
Red	People in red frequency class have excellent endurance and should choose exercises that nourish this aspect of their frequency. Since they are often slow to get going in the morning, they should consider exercising after they are warmed up. Typically, red people prefer exercises such as walking, running, cycling, and swimming. They tend to enjoy exercises and activities they do on their own. Reds may also enjoy yoga if it is strenuous enough to take advantage of their endurance.
Yellow	People in yellow frequency class have a balance of good endurance and good muscular strength. Like reds, they may gravitate toward activities such as running, walking, and swimming, or they may be drawn to team activities such as volleyball, basketball, and hockey. If a yellow scores closer to green than red in the frequency profile, then they may prefer activities with a competitive focus. If a yellow scores closer to red in the frequency profile, then they might prefer more individual exercises or activities.
Green	People in green frequency class tend to be competitive and enjoy team sports or sports and activities with some purpose or goal. People in this class tend to have excellent physical skills and should participate in sports such as recreational soccer, basketball, hockey, and competitive running—but they must make sure that one of their goals is to have *fun*. There is a risk that greens will become too competitive and focused.
Blue	People in blue frequency class are a blend of green and violet. If a blue scores closer to green than violet in the frequency profile, then they might be more interested in activities with a competitive or team-based focus. If a blue scores closer to violet in the frequency profile, then they might be more interested in activities that are social and do not necessarily have a competitive focus.
Violet	People in violet frequency class tend to fidget and have trouble focusing on any one activity for too long. They naturally move their bodies all the time, so activities that take advantage of this are recommended. Violets are drawn to activities such as yoga, dance, Pilates, and aerobics. Since people in this class are naturally extroverted, they enjoy a group atmosphere and enjoy activities that allow them to move their bodies in a variety of directions and patterns. These types of activities also help mitigate their short attention spans.

An Exercise

The above descriptions are based on the observations and interviews of many years. You may find that your preferential exercise to be different from any listed above. In the table below, describe your preferred type of exercise.

Table 18. Your Preferred Exercise

Your Base Frequency	Preferred Types of Exercise

Case Study

At the Ekahi Health Center, I recently evaluated a patient complaining of chronic shin pain from years of running. This patient had actually been relatively inactive for many years; he had been trying to return to running when an old injury returned. He had used to be a competitive runner but had been forced to quit due to chronic shin splints (general shin pain) that never improved. After he quit running, he had tried to stay active by playing hockey. While this sport was acceptable for his shins, he never really enjoyed the team atmosphere and didn't appreciate the competitiveness. He eventually stopped exercising altogether. After nearly ten years of relative inactivity, he had gone from being a very fit man to an overweight, middle-aged man with high blood pressure, chronic fatigue, and depression. He clearly needed exercise to deal with these problems.

I completed a clinical frequency profile on the patient. The clinical frequency profile is similar to the frequency profile you have already completed, but it is more in-depth and takes advantage of high-tech equipment. It was clear that the patient was a red frequency class with extremely low amplitude. I prescribed him a program that included daily meditation and a diet emphasizing raw fruits and vegetables and antioxidants. I instructed him to avoid foods typically not good for people of red frequency class. In addition, I told him to get back to exercising. I asked him at what time of day he most felt like exercising. He replied that he liked to exercise around eleven in the morning, but at that time of day he was working.

I advised the patient to change his lunch hour to eleven so he could exercise. Since he had shin pain, I asked him to start out with brisk walking for forty-five minutes every day. He would then eat his lunch at his desk when he returned to work. He was to ensure that he ate every three to four hours and drank adequate amounts of water and green tea. I also told him to schedule twenty minutes every evening for mediation focusing on self-healing and positive affirmations.

Six weeks later, my patient had reduced his blood pressure, lost twelve pounds, and was exercising with no pain. He also noted that he had much less fatigue and was optimistic about his continued improvement. He wanted to lose twenty more pounds and start to return to running. Six months after my initial meeting with the patient, he had achieved all his goals and was running two days a week and walking the other five.

Brett Wade, PhD

In Summary

- Try exercises that are suitable for your frequency class.
- Exercise when you are at your warmest or at the time of day when you feel the best.
- Exercise every day for at least twenty minutes.
- Incorporate a variety of activities into your exercise program.
- Make sure whatever activity you do resonates with your body.
- It is not unusual for your activity preferences to change as you age.

CHAPTER 18

Resonance with the Environment and Sleep

Now I see the secret of making the best person: it is to grow in the open air and to eat and sleep with the earth.
—*Walt Whitman*

A major part of nourishing your *base frequency* is making sure that your environment is in harmony with your frequency. In chapter 7, we saw how electrosmog can create an unhealthy environment. In this chapter, we will look at ways of creating a healthy environment at home and/or work that nourishes your frequency. In addition to looking at the effects of sound, music, and EMR on our environment, we will examine how colors, smells, feng shui, texture, clutter, temperature, and more affect our environment and our base frequency. I will discuss the importance of sleep and ways to ensure you are getting the best sleep possible.

An Exercise

Close your eyes and imagine a place in nature that you would describe as serene, relaxing, calming, and that makes you happy.

What does that place look like?
Example: I can see a white-sand beach with turquoise water, palm trees, and gentle rolling waves.

_____
_____

Now close your eyes again and picture that place. What sounds do you hear?
Example: I can hear waves breaking on the beach, the sound of a gentle breeze moving through the trees, and seagulls' cries.

_____
_____

Now close your eyes and picture that place again, this time adding those sounds. What do you feel?
Example: I can feel the warmth of the sun on my back, the sand under my feet, and the breeze against my skin.

_____
_____

Now close your eyes and once again imagine your place of serenity, including the sounds and sensations. What can you smell?
Example: I can smell gardenias, coconuts, and mangos.

_____
_____

What was the purpose of that exercise? Besides helping you create a perfect scene for meditation, it helped you find out what your ideal serene setting would look, sound, feel, smell, and taste like. It would be nice to be able to spend the rest of our lives in this setting, but not practical. One of the things that makes our mental retreats special is that they are places we have never been or places we only go once in a while, and therefore more of a treat.

So, back to the purpose of the exercise: Why did I ask you to visualize a place in nature? The gift of nature is the fact that it is *natural*. Nature does not consciously or unconsciously change its frequency. Nature's frequency merely responds to the environment. Even looking at nature pleases us because it contains so many examples of unforced balance. Everything has a purpose and nothing ever seems out of place—until we come along and mess it up, that is. Of course, not everything man builds is unpleasant or unnatural. A good architect, artist, or builder knows to try recreating nature and to insert their creation as naturally as possible into the environment.

Nature is soothing because it is free of noises that we find irritating or stressful. In my natural setting, there are no sirens or alarms, no sounds of engines, cars, appliances, or power tools—no sounds created by man. Again, beautiful man made sounds certainly exist, such as music by Mozart, Bach, and Vivaldi, but nothing rivals the sounds of nature for calming a nervous system.

The same goes for smells. In my natural setting, there are the smells of nature going about its business of just being. Even the smells of decomposition like algae on the beach or decaying trees in a forest are beautiful to me. In contrast, man-made smells like car exhaust, manufactured perfume, cleaning products, burning plastic, and roofing tar smell unnatural and cause a significant shift in the natural zone of my base frequency.

Now let's take this knowledge and put it to practical use by looking at the environment where you spend most of your time. For most of you, this will be your home. How can you bring some elements of your serene, natural setting into your home, or at least into one room of your home?

Brett Wade, PhD

Feng Shui

Over three thousand years old, *feng shui* is an ancient Chinese practice of orienting buildings, and translates to "wind-water." Many Taoist Chinese believe these two elements are important to good health and good fortune, and that a balance of wind and water is necessary to allow the flow of *chi*, or energy. Since both of these elements have flow, feng shui is about respecting the flow of nature and energy in our lives. Feng shui recognizes that everything has chi, including furniture like beds, lamps, dressers, sofas, etc., and that their arrangement affects the flow of energy.

The Ekahi Method views everything in life as an interaction of waves. Waves, as we have learned, are electromagnetic or mechanical waves. Since all living and nonliving things emit, at the least, infrared radiation, it stands to reason that feng shui fits into the Ekahi Method. In other words, since your sofa and coffee table emit infrared radiation, they must also interact with your base frequency. We can consider *chi* to be synonymous with *waves*.

Dr. Brett Says

- As you know, the Ekahi Method is about waves. Both living and nonliving sources emit energy. Also, waves interact with one another and, in some cases, may cause constructive interference or destructive interference. It should be no surprise that nonliving objects in our environment can affect our energy. I have helped many clients suffering from chronic diseases by using principles of feng shui to adjust the energy flow in their environments. In some cases, by just rearranging furniture in a bedroom, I have seen significant improvements in clients' ability to reset to base frequency.

An Exercise

In this exercise, we will explore ways to bring some nature and flow of waves into your bedroom. Consider each of the following factors.

Appearance: We are not trying to literally recreate your envisioned serene natural environment, but we are going to see if your room has any natural qualities.

- Clutter: Nature never clutters itself. It knows the importance of space for wind and light to flow. Get rid of anything that is not necessary.
- Space: You should have adequate room to walk on either side of and around the end of the bed.
- Art: It should be carefully chosen, minimal, and reflect some aspect of your natural, serene vision.
- Plants: Your space should contain, if possible, at least one, three, or five plants that reflect some aspect of your natural, serene vision.
- Color: Any color should be calming and generally monochromatic. Choose a color that reflects some aspect of your natural, serene vision.
- Electronics: If possible, remove or hide all electronics in the room. When you are sleeping, you should not see any power lights from televisions, DVD players, computers, etc.
- Light: Light should be controllable to reflect what is going on outside. In the morning and afternoon, windows should be opened and curtains or blinds pulled back to allow maximum light inside. At night, you should be able to create a very dark environment with blinds or curtains.
- Flow: Set things up so you can easily walk around the room.

Arrangement and Flow: Arrange things in accordance you're your observations of nature, which understands balance and flow.

- Bed: The bed should be placed in such a way that you can walk around either side and the end of the bed. Also, it should not be placed in direct alignment with the door.
- Doors: At night, keep all doors shut, including closet doors. Many plants and flowers close themselves up at night, too.
- Balance: When possible, seek balance in the bedroom with things like nightstands; try for one on each side.

Sounds: You do not generally want any electronics in your bedroom, but a portable music player can be useful for sound. For the most part, you want it to be silent, but this is almost impossible for most people to achieve.

- Music: Using a portable music player, play music or sounds which in some way reflect your natural, serene setting for fifteen to thirty minutes prior to going to sleep.
- White noise: Nature is never completely quiet. When I asked you to imagine the sounds in your natural, serene setting, you likely heard wind, water, birds or other animals, or plants or trees moving in the wind. If you have a noisy bedroom and cannot do anything about the external noise, consider adding white noise to your room. A small water fountain or a white-noise generator can be helpful especially if external noises make it difficult for you to sleep.

Smells: Remember some of the smells in your natural, serene environment. Smells are extremely powerful and must be used judiciously. More and more people these days describe themselves as chemically sensitive. Your sense of smell has a direct connection to your limbic system; therefore, smells can trigger memories.

- Outside air: If you live somewhere without strong, negative smells, open the windows to your room as much as possible.
- Flowers or plants: Plants will provide your space with oxygen, and their fragrant flowers can provide your space with a soothing atmosphere. It is also a good idea to regularly purchase cut flowers whose fragrance you enjoy for your space.
- Candles, essential oils, and incense: If your room doesn't have adequate light for plants, or if you are looking for smell sources you can change at will, try candles, incense, and essential oils, which can provide a room with a soothing aroma to help with relaxation. If you are not sure what aromas are right for you, remember that at www.ekahimethod.com we have candles and body sprays customized for each base frequency class.

Textures: With fabrics, bedding, pillows, mats, and flooring, you can create a piece of your natural, serene environment. If changing the flooring from carpet to bamboo is not in your budget, here are some things to consider:

- Bedding and fabrics: This is a nice way to incorporate not only some color from your natural, serene vision, but also some texture. Natural fibers such as silk or cotton are a nice texture for sheets and bedding.
- Mats or flooring: A mat at the foot of the bed is a nice anchor for the bed and also a good way to incorporate some textures to match your vision. Bamboo or wool mats can add a natural texture to the room.

Electrosmog: In chapter 7 we discussed how the infinite waves of ELF or UHF radiation that flow through your body may be harmful to your health. The research about health effects of ELF and UHF is contentious, but there is a significant research (Schmid et al., 2012) that shows that exposure to ELF can cause brain entrainment (synchronizing of brain waves). This means that exposure to ELF magnetic fields that have similar frequency to brain waves can actually affect your brainwave activity and thereby affect your body's natural ability to flow through the sleep cycles. If it is possible, try to make the following changes in your environment:

- Cords and transformers: Transformers plug into outlets and emit strong magnetic fields in the ELF range. If you have extension cords behind your bed, either move them or unplug them before sleep.
- Clock radios: These are big emitters of strong ELF magnetic fields. Try to move them at least five feet away from the head of the bed.
- Wireless routers and baby monitors: If possible, turn your router off at night. If you need to use a baby monitor, consider finding an on-demand monitor. These monitors only emit radiation when the receivers pick up sound.
- See chapter 8 for Dr. Brett's Top Five Mitigation Tips for ELF and UHF.
- Other mitigation techniques: If you live in an apartment building and you are electromagnetically sensitive, you might consider painting your room with EMF-blocking paint. You could apply a coat of this paint as a base and then paint over if in your preferred color.

In Summary

- Your environment is an important consideration when it comes to resonance and finding your natural zone.
- Feng shui is an ancient Chinese practice of building arrangement to ensure energy flows in your environment for health and prosperity.

- Think about environments that make you happy and serene and ask yourself how you can bring these elements into your home.
- The Ekahi Method and the philosophy of the flow of waves can be useful for learning to place objects so as to encourage the flow of energy
- Everything from arrangement, flow, colors, and smells can affect resonance.
- Everything in your environment should have a purpose and work to bring you toward your natural zone.
- Bring nature, water, and the flow of waves into your home.

Healing with Waves

CHAPTER 19

Light Waves for Health

"Healing," Papa would tell me, "is not a science, but the intuitive art of wooing nature."
—W. H. Auden

This chapter discusses the use of light to treat and prevent disease. When we hear the word *light* we usually think of the light that we can see, but recall from chapter 1 that visible light makes up only a small fraction of the electromagnetic spectrum. In fact, the whole spectrum—radio waves, microwaves, infrared rays, ultraviolet rays, x-rays, cosmic rays, and gamma rays—are all forms of light. These are all waves of energy with frequency (which is inverse to wavelength and amplitude, and they are composed of particles called photons. The expression *wave-particle duality* means that light has the properties of both waves and particles.

The respective components of visible light—red, orange, yellow, blue, indigo, and violet—definitely have effects on people. Some people are drawn to certain colors; some people are repulsed by certain colors. Our preferences of color are largely learned and cultural, but still, for many people, color can change mood. Remember that your base frequency class color has nothing to do with your favorite color. I have conducted research looking for any correlation between heart rate and breathing rate and favorite color, and I have concluded that no significant relationship exists.

How else can color be used? Color can elevate or depress our energy in the same way than does. In the previous chapter, I recommended that your bedroom contain some element of color reflecting a place in your mind which you consider serene. Color, like all light, has a frequency and photons—it has energy. Your life and your environment should provide you with a range of colors that can naturally elevate and depress your energy. Sometimes, after a busy day, you want the colors in your space to have a calming effect.

The Ekahi Method does not prescribe when choices are available. As with diet and exercise, you must determine which colors provide you with peace and which colors energize you. Most people agree that energizing colors should be placed in the kitchen. Your bedroom should contain colors that settle your energy. In the same manner, consider the other rooms of your house or living space. What do you use the room for? Should it be an energizing or relaxing place? My living room is a place for reading and listening to music, so I painted the walls cornflower-blue, an incredibly calming yet inspiring color for me.

Light Intensity and Melatonin

White light is all the colors of the rainbow put together. If you have ever seen a prism, you will have noticed that all the colors of the rainbow are revealed as the prism refracts and splits white light to show its individual wavelengths. White light is what we use to light our homes and offices when the sun has gone down or daylight is not bright enough for our purposes. While electricity has afforded us many advantages, it is my opinion that having bright white light shine on us late in the evening is unnatural and probably unhealthy.

The advent of electricity, allowing lights to be used throughout the night, has been a boon to businesses wanting to increase productivity since the industrial age. However, the advantages have likely come at the expense of our health.

If we were to really honor our circadian rhythm and base frequency rhythm, we would start dimming the lights later in the day in accordance to our rhythms so that by the time we were ready for sleep, we would be in complete darkness. Without the luxury of electricity, we might light a candle in the dark to provide enough light to be safe and to sit and listen.

The problem with electric lights, which do not naturally dim according to our natural base frequency cycles, is that they affect our hormones. We evolved from ancestors who lived according to the sun's daily cycle and to seasonal rhythms—we should still be living the same way. Electricity is a relatively new technology. Thomas Edison invented the light bulb and integrated electrical system only about 150 years ago. Before there was electricity to light incandescent bulbs, people used gas and oil lamps and candles to light their evenings. Oil and wax were limited, so people were judicious with their use of light. Now that we have relatively cheap and seemingly endless supplies of electricity, we keep the lights on all night long.

The pineal gland of the brain produces the neuroendocrine hormone melatonin in the light of the day and releases it as our environment darkens; this is a signal to begin sleeping. Besides helping to regulate our sleep cycle, melatonin is also to immunity. Research shows that exposure to nocturnal light is associated with increased risk of cancer (Bartsch, Bartsch, & Peschke, 2008). We have discussed free radicals already in this book. Melatonin is a powerful free-radical scavenger. Some research has suggested that melatonin prevent many cancers through its antioxidant effects (D. Mediavilla, J. Sanchez-Barcelo, X. Tan, Manchester, & J. Reiter, 2010).

Start turning the lights down when the sun begins to decrease in its intensity. Try to sleep in a completely darkened room. The darker the room, more melatonin will be released.

Seasonal Affective Disorder (SAD)

What can happen if we don't get enough light in the day? We have already talked about melatonin, which is produced when light strikes the retina of the eye and sends a signal to the pineal gland in the brain. When melatonin production and release are low—this can often happen in the winter months to people living in northern latitudes such as the northern United States, Canada, the United Kingdom, Scandinavia, northern Europe, and Russia—people may suffer from *seasonal affective disorder* (SAD).

The problem is not just that melatonin production is low; bright light, the trigger for the body to stop releasing melatonin, is diminished. Essentially, this means that sufferers of SAD have levels of melatonin that are low and not cycling normally (big release during the night and production during the day). A form of treatment for SAD that has been proven to be very effective is for SAD sufferers to expose their faces to bright light (Lewy, Lefler, Emens, & Bauer, 2006) with the aid of light boxes. Some of these lights are full-spectrum (white), and others are blue; research does not definitively prove that one is better than the other. Light exposure for at least thirty minutes a day in the morning helps shut off the release of melatonin and allows a person to feel more awake. Melatonin supplementation may be beneficial for those find it hard to have restorative sleep.

Dr. Brett Says

- I have treated many patients suffering from different chronic diseases. As discussed in chapter 15, vitamin D is extremely potent in its ability to help prevent many diseases. Vitamin D must be taken in either via foods high in vitamin D, and as a supplement. The body can synthesize vitamin D in the presence of ultraviolet B light. One of the most effective prescriptions I have ever written was, "Walk every day in the sunshine. If the sun is behind clouds, walk anyway—around midday or whenever your base frequency tells you it is right."

Not All Color Is Created Equal

As I have mentioned, blue light has the most intense frequency of visible light. Blocking any blue light a couple of hours before bedtime may help you get a better night's sleep. Wearing amber-tinted glasses has been shown to improve quality of sleep because, by blocking out blue light, it prepares the body by creating a "physiological darkness" (Burkhart & Phelps, 2009). Blocking blue light stimulates the body to start releasing stored melatonin from the pineal gland; this creates a feeling of relaxation and sleepiness, like eating a turkey dinner. In fact, tryptophan, which is found in turkey and chicken and can make you sleepy, is an amino acid that can be eventually converted to melatonin.

The reason that the color amber blocks blue light is that amber and blue are complementary colors; their two frequencies combined leads to destructive interference which drastically reduces the intensity of the blue light.

Ultraviolet Light, Vitamin D, and Health

Ultraviolet radiation can also be used to treat SAD. If you live in a latitude or climate where the sun shines brightly even in winter, you will be getting enough of it from the sun. But if you live in a latitude or climate where the winter months do not afford an appreciable amount of sunlight during the day, you should supplement with vitamin D.

Technically, another way to increase vitamin D biosynthesis is to use a tanning bed that contains both UVA and UVB rays—most do. But the use of tanning beds to increase the body's ability to produce vitamin D is controversial. Numerous studies have shown a significant increase in skin cancer with the use of tanning beds, particularly for young people (Berwick, 2008; Brady, 2012; Woo & Eide, 2010).

One problem with relying solely on UVA and UVB exposure to increase vitamin D synthesis is that, in order for your skin cells to produce melanin (the pigment which gives you a tan), a type of skin cell call keratinocytes must be radiated to cause DNA damage. This in turn causes an inflammatory reaction and, finally, increased melanin deposited into the keratinocyte (Brady, 2012). This type of radiation is, therefore, ionizing. Most tanning beds use mainly UVA (UVA is approximately 90 to 95 percent of the total UV radiation) and very little UVB. However, UVB is the only ultraviolet frequency which can lead to a tan. UVA was once thought to be noncarcinogenic, but recent research has found that UVA is related to skin cancer (Woo & Eide, 2010).

Infrared Radiation and Saunas

Recently the use of infrared light in saunas has been purported by manufacturers to treat diseases, induce weight loss, prevent diseases, and more. Infrared radiation is nonionizing and its wavelength is just beyond the visible light of the color red. Infrared radiation is emitted by the sun, just as all frequencies of the electromagnetic spectrum (both ionizing and nonionizing) are, and it is detected as heat. Most of the radiation we experience on the surface of the earth is, in fact, infrared. The infrared radiation closest in frequency to the visible spectrum is known as near-infrared, whereas the infrared radiation closest to microwaves (cell phone frequencies) is known as far-infrared, or very-long wave infrared (see figure 28).

The Ekahi Method

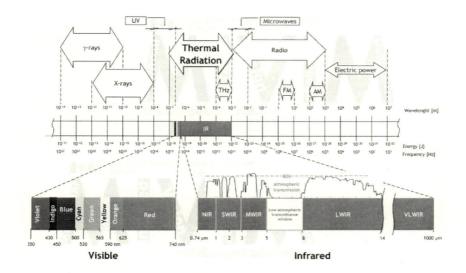

Figure 28. Infrared Radiation Spectrum
Ibarrac at en.wikipedia [CC-BY-SA-3.0 (http://creativecommons.org/licenses/by-sa/3.0) or GFDL (http://www.gnu.org/copyleft/fdl.html)], from Wikimedia Commons

There are both near-infrared and far-infrared saunas available on the market. While various manufacturers make claims that their type of infrared sauna is superior, the way each type of sauna delivers heat is quite different. Near-infrared saunas radiate heat from an infrared lamp at frequencies just slightly lower than those of visible red light (see NIR in figure 28). Far-infrared saunas generate heat by emitting microwave radiation, which has low frequencies (see VLWIR in figure 28) and causes internal heating in the body by stimulating thermal receptors in the skin.

As you may remember from chapter 2, frequency determines the depth of penetration of waves. The lower the frequency of the wave (radio waves, for example), the more easily it passes right through us. The higher the frequency, the harder it is for the wave to penetrate the skin. Infrared radiation has the right electromagnetic frequency to penetrate the skin and stimulate thermal receptors and sensory nerves. Ultraviolet radiation, on the other hand, has a higher frequency and only penetrates a small depth into the skin. Depth of penetration is not entirely dependent on wave frequency. The energy contained in a wave's photons also determines whether the wave will be absorbed by certain tissues or pass right through them. X-rays are a good example of a high-frequency wave that passes through skin, fat, and muscle, but is absorbed by bone.

Near-Infrared Vs. Far-Infrared

There is endless debate over which one electromagnetic frequency is better for heating saunas, but suffice it to say, both types generate heat. There is also debate over which frequency penetrates more deeply and has a greater heating effect. At the end of the day, both near- and far- infrared radiation generate frequencies that the body experiences as heat. Both forms of infrared radiation are nonionizing and should technically, therefore, be safe. It has been suggested that it takes more power to generate far-infrared radiation, so a far-infrared-sauna user might absorb more electromagnetic radiation.

Does Research Support Infrared-Sauna Use?

A recent study (Oosterveld et al., 2009) showed temporary improvement of pain levels in people with rheumatoid arthritis and ankylosing spondylitis when treated with infrared saunas for four weeks, two times a week. A study in *Canadian Family Physician* (Beever, 2009) reviewed the research on far-infrared saunas and found that, overall, while there are very few studies that support their use for medical conditions, there is moderate support for the use of far-infrared saunas in treating high blood pressure and congestive heart failure.

There are several poorly designed studies and anecdotal reports that make numerous claims about the beneficial effects of infrared saunas, but most of those claims are unsubstantiated.

Low-Power Lasers for Tissue Healing

Laser is an acronym that stands for *L*ight *A*mplification *S*timulated *E*mission of *R*adiation. Low-power lasers, also called cold lasers, are gaining popularity in clinical use for the treatment of soft tissue injuries such as sprains and strains. A low-power laser works by running an electric current through a medium such as a combination of helium (He) and neon (Ne), or gallium (Ga) and arsenide (As). The electric current excites the atoms, which causes the release of a photon from one of the atoms' electrons. This photon will then energize the next atom, causing a chain reaction and the release of photons of specific frequency and energy. Lasers that emit light of wavelengths between 600 and 1,300 nanometers (nm) will stimulate tissue just under half a centimeter in depth (Cameron, 2003). HeNe lasers emit visible red light (630 nm), whereas GaAs emit infrared radiation (830 nm).

As with most forms of electromagnetic radiation, lower-frequency waves (which have longer wavelengths) penetrate deeper. The clinical use of cold lasers such as HeNe and GaAs lasers have been shown to be beneficial in the treatment of tissue and wound healing by increasing collagen synthesis (Enwemeka et al., 2004; Hopkins, McLoda, Seegmiller, & David Baxter, 2004). Cold lasers have also been shown to help in chronic-pain relief (Gur et al., 2003; Walker, 1983) and they have shown promise in the treatment of hair loss (Avram & Rogers, 2009).

Case Study

> A patient with significant pain in her right knee came to see me for relief of her symptoms. The patient had moderate to advanced osteoarthritis of the knee. There was palpable swelling around the knee joint and a lack of full movement when bending the knee. I made some

recommendations about proper exercises, such as cycling and swimming, and also to help her lower her weight, which would decrease forces in her knee joint. In addition, I started her on GaAs-laser treatment at two sessions per week for six weeks. After her laser treatment, she had a significant reduction in pain and improved range of motion in her knee.

In Summary

- Ultraviolet, visible, and infrared light can be both harmful and helpful for healing and health.
- Exposure to sunlight for at least thirty minutes a day helps in the production of melatonin and vitamin D.
- If you live in a low latitude and suffer from SAD, you should consider supplementing with melatonin and vitamin D and using a light box in the mornings. Also, wearing amber lenses a few hours before bed may trigger the release of melatonin.
- Infrared saunas may be of some benefit for temporary pain relief.
- Low-level lasers are clinically proven to increase wound healing and decrease pain.

CHAPTER 20

Healing with Electromagnetism and Ultrasound

Adopt the pace of nature: her secret is patience.
—Ralph Waldo Emerson

We saw in chapter 19 how light between ultraviolet and infrared frequencies can be used for healing soft tissue injuries and improving health. Clinical low-level lasers can be used to for conditions such as muscle strain, ligament sprain, tendon injury, and arthritis pain. Infrared saunas may help with temporary relief of pain, and ultraviolet and blue light can treat SAD. Now we will discuss how extremely low frequency (ELF) electromagnetic radiation and the mechanical waves of ultrasound can be used to heal and treat certain conditions.

Recall from chapter 2 that ELF radiation is nonioninzing radiation with the longest wavelengths and the lowest frequency (figure 4). Besides the sun, there are many sources of ELF in our environment, such as overhead power lines, household electrical wiring, and appliances. The frequency of ELF radiation covers the spectrum, from 3 Hz to 300 Hz.

A natural source of ELF radiation is the regular lightning discharges around the planet; these create a background frequency called

Schumann resonances. Fluctuations in the earth's magnetic field can also enter into ELF ranges. In previous chapters, we discussed the potential negative health effects associated with ELF radiation exposure. While research is inconclusive, there are established mechanisms which could explain some of the positive correlations between ELF and disease. ELF radiation from wiring and appliances is the result of an alternating current of 50 Hz in most of Europe and 60 Hz in North America. This flow of alternating current creates an electromagnetic field.

ELF Radiation for Healing

Research has shown that there can be benefits to exposure to ELF radiation of much lower frequency and lower magnetic field strength—in many cases, a thousand times less—than that of the ambient field in a typical North American home. Pulsed electromagnetic fields (PEMF) have been used for nearly a century; they were a common modality used by physicians of the early 1900s for wound healing and the treatment of a wide range of conditions. PEMF is making a comeback, and research supports its clinical use.

PEMF is the external application of a pulsing electromagnetic field of low frequency (usually less than 75 Hz) and weak magnetic field. Research has found the following conditions respond favorably to the application of PEMF (table 19):

Table 19. Conditions Which Respond Favorably to PEMF

Condition	Reference(s)
Multiple sclerosis	(Richards et al., 1997)
Osteoarthritis of the knee	(Pipitone & Scott, 2001)
Fibromyalgia	(Sutbeyaz, Sezer, Koseoglu, & Kibar, 2009)

Loosened hip prosthesis	(Kennedy, Roberts, Zuege, & Dicus, 1993)
Cervical osteoarthritis	(Sutbeyaz, Sezer, & Koseoglu, 2006)
Lateral epicondylitis (tennis elbow)	(Uzunca, Birtane, & Tastekin, 2007)
Pain of rheumatoid arthritis and fibromyalgia	(Shupak et al., 2006)
Congenital pseudoarthrosis	(Bassett & Schink-Ascani, 1991)
Cervical and knee pain due to osteoarthritis	(Trock, Bollet, & Markoll, 1994)
Delayed union tibial fractures	(Sharrard, 1990)
Chronic rotator cuff tendinitis	(Binder, Parr, Hazleman, & Fitton-Jackson, 1984)
Osteoporosis	(Huang, He, He, Chen, & Yang, 2008)
Osteonecrosis of the hip	(Yoo, Cho, Kim, Chun, & Chung, 2004)
Chronic venous ulcers	(Stiller et al., 1992)

While it is not completely clear to us how PEMF works, the following table (table 20) describes some of the cellular mechanisms of PEMF.

Table 20. The Cellular Effects of PEMF Exposure

Cell Type	Mechanism	PEMF parameters	References
Chondrocytes (cartilage cells)	Increased number of chondrocytes	75 Hz, 2.3 mT	(Mattei et al., 2001)
Osteoblasts (bone cells)	Increased proliferation of osteoblasts	15 Hz, 0.1 mT	(Chang, Chen, Sun, & Lin, 2004)
Neutrophils (white blood cells)	Saturated adenosine receptors leading to decreased inflammatory cytokine cascade	75 Hz, 0.2mT-3.5mT	(Varani et al., 2002)

Mononuclear cells	Significant increases in IL-1β and TNF-α (pro-inflammatory cytokines)	50 Hz, 2.25 mT	(Gómez-Ochoa, Gómez-Ochoa, Gómez-Casal, Cativiela, & Larrad-Mur, 2011)
Fibroblasts	Reduction of cAMP leading to increased proliferation of collagen cells	15 Hz, 4.8 ms-pulse	(Farndale & Murray, 1985)
Endothelial cells	Increased proliferation of endothelial cells leading to angiogenesis	50 Hz, 1mT	(Delle Monache, Alessandro, Iorio, Gualtieri, & Colonna, 2008)

In addition to these cellular effects, it is thought that PEMF facilitates the movement of ions across the cell membrane. Ions such as sodium (Na^+), potassium (K^+), calcium (Ca^{2+}), and chlorine (Cl^-) are very important for actions in the cell such as causing nerves to send signals, making of DNA, producing energy, and much more. PEMF may cause ions to move into cell membranes, in essence, increasing cell metabolism of the cell and thus, healing.

Since the frequencies used by PEMF are between those of the earth's magnetic field (which essentially has no frequency) and the Schumann resonances, PEMF frequencies appear to be natural to humans. In most PEMF treatments, either a body mat (figure 29) or a small pad or coil is used to deliver the magnetic field. Most people cannot feel anything while the treatment is in session.

Who Offers PEMF?

If you are considering the use of PEMF, see a licensed physical therapist who is familiar with using this modality. Other health care practitioners who might use this modality include chiropractors, naturopathic physicians, and other alternative-health-care providers.

The Ekahi Method

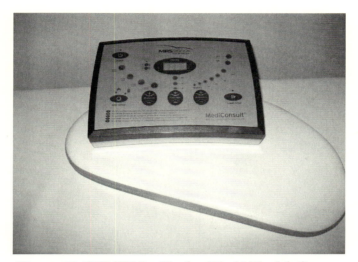

Figure 29. PEMF Mat Used at Ekahi Health Centre

Case Study

A patient came into the Ekahi Method Health Center suffering from significant fatigue related to multiple sclerosis. I suggested a six-week trial of PEMF. On his first assessment, the patient reported his fatigue over the past month as very high (50 out of 63). After the full course of treatment, the patient had more energy and was now at 35 on the fatigue scale—a very significant improvement.

Static Magnets

Proponents of static magnets treat a variety of ailments by placing magnets in shoes or mattresses or on areas of the body. There is some research demonstrating efficacy of static magnets in treating arthritis (Hinman, Ford, & Heyl, 2002; Wolsko et al., 2004), pain (Eccles, 2005), diabetic neuropathy (Weintraub et al., 2003), or pelvic pain (Brown, Ling, Wan, & Pilla, 2002). One study reviewed a number of other studies on this subject. Although it was not a comprehensive review of the relevant literature, it does suggest that static magnets may be of some benefit to pain reduction. However, the study also reported that over 60 percent of the reviewed studies did not contain enough details about experiment design to be effectively evaluated (Colbert et al., 2009). Research shows many conflicting findings about the use of static magnetic fields. Since static magnets do not have an alternating field, they do not create waves, and as such, are not part of the focus of this book.

Ultrasound Waves for Tissue Healing

The frequency of the sound waves that we can hear ranges from 30 Hz to 20 kHz. In the early 1900s, it was discovered that sound waves could be used to listen surreptitiously for enemies through the use of sonar. In the 1920s, it was discovered that ultrasonic waves (very high, inaudible frequencies and high intensities) could be used to destroy gallstones. This is called lithotripsy and is still today one of the most effective ways of treating gallstones.

In the 1930s, scientists discovered that decreasing the intensity of the ultrasound gave it therapeutic effects, including tissue healing. The frequencies of therapeutic ultrasound are between 0.75 MHz and 3 MHz. These high frequencies are well beyond what the human ear can detect. When these sound waves pass through the skin, they can penetrate approximately three centimeters deep (Hayes, Merrick, Sandrey, & Cordova, 2004). These mechanical sound waves can be adjusted to deliver a wave intensity (2.0 W/cm^2) that can heat tissue by vibrating molecules in the area. When much lower intensities are used (0.1 W/cm^2 to 1.0 W/cm^2), ultrasounds can have nonthermal effects such as effectively speeding up tissue healing by increasing protein synthesis, increasing local calcium-ion concentration, and increasing local blood vessel formation (Dyson, 1982).

Conditions Shown to Benefit from Therapeutic Ultrasound

Animal studies have shown ultrasound to improve fracture healing (Warden et al., 2006) and nerve regeneration (Mourad et al., 2001). There is also support for the use of ultrasound in wound healing (Kavros, Miller, & Hanna, 2007; Uhlemann, Heinig, & Wollina, 2003).

While therapeutic ultrasound has been used extensively used for decades, research suggests that its greatest clinical effect may be in treating fractures that are resistant to healing and chronic wounds such as diabetic ulcers, and in speeding up nerve regeneration after a nerve has been damaged.

Who Offers Therapeutic Ultrasound?

Historically, therapeutic ultrasound was predominantly offered by physical therapists. Now, however, a chiropractor, naturopathic physician, or other alternative-health-care provider may offer this service.

Dr. Brett Says

- If you decide to try PEMF, ultrasound, or low-power lasers, know that these modalities in themselves are unlikely to cure any disease. Research has shown them to be useful adjuncts to healing in some cases, but one should never be deceived into thinking that these modalities alone will cure disease.

In Summary

- The use of PEMF has been shown to be effective in treating many conditions.

- The use of therapeutic ultrasound may of some benefit for bone-fracture healing, nerve regeneration, and wound healing
- If you are considering the use of either of these modalities, speak to a qualified health care practitioner for their opinion.

CONCLUSION

Master the Waves of Life

*You must live in the present, launch yourself on every wave,
find your eternity in each moment.*
—Henry David Thoreau

Thank you for learning to ride the waves with me. The Ekahi Method sees all of life as connected by one thing: waves. Most people bump through their way, never understanding the indisputable fact that all of life interacts by the exchange of energy on a wave.

We started off learning the concept of waves and how they comprise everything in life, and we learned new terms (the natural zone, constructive interference, destructive interference, wave reducers, and wave amplifiers). You completed the frequency profile to determine your base frequency color. You were taught about how the base frequencies of objects and people interact with your own by either wave reducing, wave amplifying, or pulling you out of your base frequency. You must reset to your base frequency through daily meditation. Then you can learn how to tune, or adjust your base frequency to that of other people to temporarily improve a situation. Regarding decision making, intuition is essentially a small vibration or wave created by thought. Then you learned how to honor and nourish your base frequency with resonant food, music, and exercise. Finally, we looked at some types of waves that can be used for treating healing certain medical conditions: sound waves, PEMF, cold lasers, and ultraviolet/infrared/full-spectrum light.

To master the waves of life, you need to put all the knowledge you have gained over the course of this book into practice. It takes time and practice to achieve mastery of something. I stated at the beginning of the book that if you practice the Ekahi Method for six weeks, you will start to see changes in your life. In order to achieve mastery of the five parts of the Ekahi Method, you need only regularly practice what you have learned. If you are having trouble starting the method or maintaining it, then the most important thing you can do is to commit to daily meditation. By just resetting to your base frequency with this simple act, you will start to unleash the full potential of the Ekahi Method.

It is important to remember that life is a wave; there will always be ups and downs. Once we learn to master the waves of life, we are less likely to become overwhelmed by its constant, universal energy. The Ekahi Method came to me during meditation. I was feeling lost, scared, and deeply depressed about my direction in life. I knew that the one thing I could control at that moment was the decision to meditate and try to center myself. This meditation session would prove to be the most profound and meaningful one of my life. I sat for over two hours writing the book in my head. Then I got up, grabbed a pen, and wrote, "There is only one thing that we need to learn: How to master the waves of life." I learned to surf the waves that day, and my life has not been the same since.

I look forward to one day meeting you out there on the waves of life.

Dr. Brett

(Visit www.ekahimethod.com to learn more about Ekahi Method services and products or to book Dr. Brett for a speaking engagement.)

REFERENCES

Antonopoulos, A., Yang, B., Stamm, A., Heller, W. D., & Obe, G. (1995). Cytological effects of 50 Hz electromagnetic fields on human lymphocytes in vitro. *Mutation Research, 346*(3), 151-157.

Ascherio, A., Munger, K. L., & Simon, K. C. (2010). Vitamin D and multiple sclerosis. *The Lancet Neurology, 9*(6), 599-612.

Avram, M. R., & Rogers, N. E. (2009). The use of low-level light for hair growth: Part I. *Journal of Cosmetic and Laser Therapy, 11*(2), 110-117.

Bartsch, C., Bartsch, H., & Peschke, E. (2008). Light, melatonin and cancer: current results and future perspectives 1. *Biological Rhythm Research, 40*(1), 17-35.

Bassett, C., & Schink-Ascani, M. (1991). Long-term pulsed electromagnetic field (PEMF) results in congenital pseudarthrosis. *Calcified Tissue International, 49*(3), 216-220.

Bates, C. (2013). Two hearts really DO beat as one if you're in love: Scientists find couples' vital signs mimic each other. *Daily Mail*.

Beever, R. (2009). Far-infrared saunas for treatment of cardiovascular risk factors: Summary of published evidence. *Canadian Family Physician, 55*(7), 691-696.

Berwick, M. (2008). Are tanning beds "safe"? Human studies of melanoma. *Pigment Cell & Melanoma Research, 21*(5), 517-519.

Bhutta, M. F. (2007). Sex and the nose: human pheromonal responses. *J R Soc Med, 100*(6), 268-274.

Bianchi, N., Crosignani, P., Rovelli, A., Tittarelli, A., Carnelli, C. A., Rossitto, F., et al. (2000). Overhead electricity power lines and childhood leukemia: a registry-based, case-control study. *Tumori, 86*(3), 195-198.

Binder, A., Parr, G., Hazleman, B., & Fitton-Jackson, S. (1984). PULSED ELECTROMAGNETIC FIELD THERAPY OF PERSISTENT ROTATOR CUFF TENDINITIS: A Double-blind Controlled Assessment. *The Lancet, 323*(8379), 695-698.

Brady, M. S. (2012). Public Health and the Tanning Bed Controversy. *Journal of Clinical Oncology, 30*(14), 1571-1573.

Brown, C. S., Ling, F. W., Wan, J. Y., & Pilla, A. A. (2002). Efficacy of static magnetic field therapy in chronic pelvic pain: A double-blind pilot study. *American Journal of Obstetrics and Gynecology, 187*(6), 1581-1587.

Burkhart, K., & Phelps, J. R. (2009). Amber lenses to block blue light and improve sleep: a randomized trial. *Chronobiol Int, 26*(8), 1602-1612.

Cameron, M. (2003). *Physical Agents in Rehabilitation - From Research to Practice* (Second ed.). Philadelphia: Elsevier Science.

Chang, W. H.-S., Chen, L.-T., Sun, J.-S., & Lin, F.-H. (2004). Effect of pulse-burst electromagnetic field stimulation on osteoblast cell activities. *Bioelectromagnetics, 25*(6), 457-465.

Chernouss, S., Vinogradov, A., & Vlassova, E. (2001). Geophysical Hazard for Human Health in the Circumpolar Auroral Belt: Evidence of a Relationship between Heart Rate Variation and Electromagnetic Disturbances. *Natural Hazards, 23*(2-3), 121-135.

Chiu, C. C., Su, K. P., Cheng, T. C., Liu, H. C., Chang, C. J., Dewey, M. E., et al. (2008). The effects of omega-3 fatty acids monotherapy in Alzheimer's disease and mild cognitive impairment: a preliminary randomized double-blind placebo-controlled study. *Progress in neuro-psychopharmacology & biological psychiatry, 32*(6), 1538-1544.

Colbert, A. P., Wahbeh, H., #xE9, Harling, N., Connelly, E., Schiffke, H. C., et al. (2009). Static Magnetic Field Therapy: A Critical Review of Treatment Parameters. *Evidence-Based Complementary and Alternative Medicine, 6*(2), 133-139.

Cook, C. M., Thomas, A. W., Keenliside, L., & Prato, F. S. (2005). Resting EEG effects during exposure to a pulsed ELF magnetic field. *Bioelectromagnetics, 26*(5), 367-376.

Correale, J., Ysrraelit, M. C., & Gaitán, M. I. (2009). Immunomodulatory effects of Vitamin D in multiple sclerosis. *Brain, 132*(5), 1146-1160.

Craft, L. L., & Perna, F. M. (2004). The Benefits of Exercise for the Clinically Depressed. *Prim Care Companion J Clin Psychiatry, 6*(3), 104-111.

Cutolo, M., Otsa, K., Uprus, M., Paolino, S., & Seriolo, B. (2007). Vitamin D in rheumatoid arthritis. *Autoimmunity Reviews, 7*(1), 59-64.

D. Mediavilla, M., J. Sanchez-Barcelo, E., X. Tan, D., Manchester, L., & J. Reiter, R. (2010). Basic Mechanisms Involved in the Anti-Cancer Effects of Melatonin. *Current Medicinal Chemistry, 17*(36), 4462-4481.

Davidson, R. J., Kabat-Zinn, J., Schumacher, J., Rosenkranz, M., Muller, D., Santorelli, S. F., et al. (2003). Alterations in Brain and Immune Function Produced by Mindfulness Meditation. *Psychosomatic Medicine, 65*(4), 564-570.

Dell'Amore, C. (2011). Your Heart Can Sync With a Loved One's *National Geographic Daily News*. Retrieved from http://news.nationalgeographic.com/news/2011/05/110504-fire-walking-hearts-beat-science-health-heartbeats/

Delle Monache, S., Alessandro, R., Iorio, R., Gualtieri, G., & Colonna, R. (2008). Extremely low frequency electromagnetic fields (ELF-EMFs) induce in vitro angiogenesis process in human endothelial cells. *Bioelectromagnetics, 29*(8), 640-648.

Dietary Reference Intakes for Calcium and Vitamin D. (2011). The National Academies Press.

Divan, H. A., Kheifets, L., Obel, C., & Olsen, J. (2008). Prenatal and Postnatal Exposure to Cell Phone Use and Behavioral Problems in Children. *Epidemiology, 19*(4), 523-529 510.1097/EDE.1090b1013e318175dd318147.

Draper, G., Vincent, T., Kroll, M. E., & Swanson, J. (2005). Childhood cancer in relation to distance from high voltage power lines in England and Wales: a case-control study. *BMJ, 330*(7503), 1290.

Dyson, M. (1982). Non-thermal cellular effects of ultrasound. *Br J Cancer Suppl, 5,* 165-171.

Eccles, N. K. (2005). A critical review of randomized controlled trials of static magnets for pain relief. *J Altern Complement Med, 11*(3), 495-509.

Electromagnetic fields and public health. (2007). *World Health Organization, Fact Sheet #322.* Retrieved from http://www.who.int/mediacentre/factsheets/fs322/en/index.html

EMF - Electric and Magnetic Fields Associated with the Use of Electric Power. (2002). *National Institute of Environmental Health Sciences. National Institutes of Health* Retrieved from http://www.niehs.nih.gov/emfrapid

Enwemeka, C. S., Parker, J. C., Dowdy, D. S., Harkness, E. E., Sanford, L. E., & Woodruff, L. D. (2004). The efficacy of low-power lasers in tissue repair and pain control: a meta-analysis study. *Photomed Laser Surg, 22*(4), 323-329.

Extremely Low Frequency Fields. (2007). *WHO: Environmental Health,* (Criteria 238),

Farndale, R., & Murray, J. (1985). Pulsed electromagnetic fields promote collagen production in bone marrow fibroblasts via athermal mechanisms. *Calcified Tissue International, 37*(2), 178-182.

Fifer, W. P., & Moon, C. M. (1994). The role of mother's voice in the organization of brain function in the newborn. *Acta Pædiatrica, 83,* 86-93.

Fontani, G., Corradeschi, F., Felici, A., Alfatti, F., Migliorini, S., & Lodi, L. (2005). Cognitive and physiological effects of Omega-3 polyunsaturated fatty acid supplementation in healthy subjects. *European Journal of Clinical Investigation, 35*(11), 691-699.

Garland, C. F., Garland, F. C., Gorham, E. D., Lipkin, M., Newmark, H., Mohr, S. B., et al. (2006). The Role of Vitamin D in Cancer Prevention. *American Journal of Public Health, 96*(2), 252-261.

Geusens, P., Wouters, C., Nijs, J., Jiang, Y., & Dequeker, J. (1994). Long-term effect of omega-3 fatty acid supplementation in active rheumatoid arthritis. *Arthritis & Rheumatism, 37*(6), 824-829.

Glerup, H., Mikkelsen, K., Poulsen, L., Hass, E., Overbeck, S., Thomsen, J., et al. (2000). Commonly recommended daily intake of vitamin D is not sufficient if sunlight exposure is limited. *Journal of Internal Medicine, 247*(2), 260-268.

Gómez-Ochoa, I., Gómez-Ochoa, P., Gómez-Casal, F., Cativiela, E., & Larrad-Mur, L. (2011). Pulsed electromagnetic fields decrease proinflammatory cytokine secretion (IL-1β and TNF-α) on human fibroblast-like cell culture. *Rheumatology International, 31*(10), 1283-1289.

Guidelines for limiting exposure to time-varying electric and magnetic fields (1 Hz to 100 kHz). (2010). *Health Phys, 99*(6), 818-836.

Gur, A., Cosut, A., Sarac, A. J., Cevik, R., Nas, K., & Uyar, A. (2003). Efficacy of different therapy regimes of low-power laser in painful osteoarthritis of the knee: a double-blind and randomized-controlled trial. *Lasers Surg Med, 33*(5), 330-338.

Harries, A. D., Brown, R., Heatley, R. V., Williams, L. A., Woodhead, S., & Rhodes, J. (1985). Vitamin D status in Crohn's disease: association with nutrition and disease activity. *Gut, 26*(11), 1197-1203.

Havas, M., Marrongelle, J., Pollner, B., Kelley, E., Rees, C. R., & Tully, L. (2010). Provocation study using heart rate variability shows microwave radiation from 2.4 GHz cordless phone affects autonomic nervous system. *Non-thermal Effects and Mechanisms of Interaction between Electromagnetic Fields and Living Matter. European Journal of Oncology Library, 5.*

Hayes, B. T., Merrick, M. A., Sandrey, M. A., & Cordova, M. L. (2004). Three-MHz Ultrasound Heats Deeper Into the Tissues Than Originally Theorized. *J Athl Train, 39*(3), 230-234.

Hillert, L., Åkerstedt, T., Lowden, A., Wiholm, C., Kuster, N., Ebert, S., et al. (2008). The effects of 884 MHz GSM wireless communication signals on headache and other symptoms: An experimental provocation study. *Bioelectromagnetics, 29*(3), 185-196.

Hinman, M. R., Ford, J., & Heyl, H. (2002). Effects of static magnets on chronic knee pain and physical function: a double-blind study. *Alternative therapies in health and medicine, 8*(4), 50-55.

Hocking, B., Gordon, I. R., Grain, H. L., & Hatfield, G. E. (1996). Cancer incidence and mortality and proximity to TV towers. *Med J Aust, 165*(11-12), 601-605.

Hölzel, B. K., Carmody, J., Vangel, M., Congleton, C., Yerramsetti, S. M., Gard, T., et al. (2011). Mindfulness practice leads to increases in regional brain gray matter density. *Psychiatry Research: Neuroimaging, 191*(1), 36-43.

Hopkins, J. T., McLoda, T. A., Seegmiller, J. G., & David Baxter, G. (2004). Low-Level Laser Therapy Facilitates Superficial Wound Healing in Humans: A Triple-Blind, Sham-Controlled Study. *J Athl Train, 39*(3), 223-229.

Hu Fb, B. L. W. W. C., & et al. (2002). FIsh and omega-3 fatty acid intake and risk of coronary heart disease in women. *JAMA, 287*(14), 1815-1821.

Huang, L. Q., He, H. C., He, C. Q., Chen, J., & Yang, L. (2008). Clinical update of pulsed electromagnetic fields on osteoporosis. *Chin Med J, 121*(20), 2095-2099.

Human Exposure to Radio Frequency Fields: Guidelines For Cellular and PCS Sites. (2011). *Federal Communications Commission*. Retrieved from http://www.fcc.gov/guides/human-exposure-rf-fields-guidelines-cellular-and-pcs-sites

Ivancsits, S., Diem, E., Pilger, A., Rudiger, H. W., & Jahn, O. (2002). Induction of DNA strand breaks by intermittent exposure to extremely-low-frequency electromagnetic fields in human diploid fibroblasts. *Mutation Research, 519*(1-2), 1-13.

Ivancsits, S., Pilger, A., Diem, E., Jahn, O., & Rudiger, H. W. (2005). Cell type-specific genotoxic effects of intermittent extremely low-frequency electromagnetic fields.[see comment]. *Mutation Research, 583*(2), 184-188.

Kabat-Zinn, J., Massion, A. O., Kristeller, J., Peterson, L. G., Fletcher, K. E., Pbert, L., et al. (1992). Effectiveness of a meditation-based stress reduction program in the treatment of anxiety disorders. *The American journal of psychiatry, 149*(7), 936-943.

Kavros, S. J., Miller, J. L., & Hanna, S. W. (2007). Treatment of Ischemic Wounds with Noncontact, Low-Frequency Ultrasound: The Mayo Clinic Experience, 2004-2006. *Advances in Skin & Wound Care, 20*(4), 221-226 210.1097/1001.ASW.0000266660.0000288900.0000266638.

Kennedy, W. F., Roberts, C. G., Zuege, R. C., & Dicus, W. T. (1993). Use of pulsed electromagnetic fields in treatment of loosened cemented hip prostheses. A double-blind trial. *Clin Orthop Relat Res, 286*(286), 198-205.

Khurana, V. G., Teo, C., Kundi, M., Hardell, L., & Carlberg, M. (2009). Cell phones and brain tumors: a review including the long-term epidemiologic data. *Surgical Neurology, 72*(3), 205-214.

Kim, T. J., Nam, K. W., Shin, H. S., Lee, S. M., Yang, J. S., & Soh, K. S. (2002). Biophoton emission from fingernails and fingerprints of living human subjects. *Acupunct Electrother Res, 27*(2), 85-94.

La, L., & German, K. (2012). Cell Phone Radiation Levels. *cnet*. Retrieved from http://reviews.cnet.com/cell-phone-radiation-levels/

Lee, J. H., O'Keefe, J. H., Bell, D., Hensrud, D. D., & Holick, M. F. (2008). Vitamin D DeficiencyAn Important, Common, and Easily Treatable Cardiovascular Risk Factor? *Journal of the American College of Cardiology, 52*(24), 1949-1956.

Lehrer, S., Green, S., & Stock, R. (2011). Association between number of cell phone contracts and brain tumor incidence in nineteen U.S. States. *Journal of Neuro-Oncology, 101*(3), 505-507.

Lewy, A. J., Lefler, B. J., Emens, J. S., & Bauer, V. K. (2006). The circadian basis of winter depression. *Proc Natl Acad Sci U S A, 103*(19), 7414-7419.

Luders, E., Toga, A. W., Lepore, N., & Gaser, C. (2009). The underlying anatomical correlates of long-term meditation: Larger hippocampal and frontal volumes of gray matter. *NeuroImage, 45*(3), 672-678.

Machado, C., Korein, J., Aubert, E., Bosch, J., Alvarez, M. A., Rodríguez, R., et al. (2007). Recognizing a Mother's Voice in the Persistent Vegetative State. *Clinical EEG and Neuroscience, 38*(3), 124-126.

Mattei, M. D., Caruso, A., Pezzetti, F., Pellati, A., Stabellini, G., Sollazzo, V., et al. (2001). Effects of Pulsed Electromagnetic Fields on Human Articular Chondrocyte Proliferation. *Connective Tissue Research, 42*(4), 269-279.

Moore, S. C., Patel, A. V., Matthews, C. E., Berrington de Gonzalez, A., Park, Y., Katki, H. A., et al. (2012). Leisure Time Physical Activity of Moderate to Vigorous Intensity and Mortality: A Large Pooled Cohort Analysis. *PLoS Med, 9*(11), e1001335.

Moss, A. S., Wintering, N., Roggenkamp, H., Khalsa, D. S., Waldman, M. R., Monti, D., et al. (2012). Effects of an 8-week meditation program on mood and anxiety in patients with memory loss. *J Altern Complement Med, 18*(1), 48-53.

Mourad, P. D., Lazar, D. A., Curra, F. P., Mohr, B. C., Andrus, K. C., Avellino, A. M., et al. (2001). Ultrasound Accelerates Functional Recovery after Peripheral Nerve Damage. *Neurosurgery, 48*(5), 1136-1141.

Mujica-Parodi, L. R., Strey, H. H., Botanov, Y., Tolkunov, D., Rubin, D., Weber, J., et al. (2009). Chemosensory Cues to Conspecific Emotional Stress Activate Amygdala in Humans. *PLoS ONE, 4*(7), e6415.

Nayak, S., Wheeler, B. L., Shiflett, S. C., & Agostinelli, S. (2000). Effect of music therapy on mood and social interaction among individuals with acute traumatic brain injury and stroke. *Rehabilitation Psychology, 45*(3), 274.

Oosterveld, F. J., Rasker, J., Floors, M., Landkroon, R., Rennes, B., Zwijnenberg, J., et al. (2009). Infrared sauna in patients with rheumatoid arthritis and ankylosing spondylitis. *Clinical Rheumatology, 28*(1), 29-34.

Pacchetti, C., Mancini, F., Aglieri, R., Fundaro, C., Martignoni, E., & Nappi, G. (2000). Active music therapy in Parkinson's disease: an integrative method for motor and emotional rehabilitation. *Psychosom Med, 62*(3), 386-393.

Panagopoulos, D. J., Karabarbounis, A., & Margaritis, L. H. (2002). Mechanism for action of electromagnetic fields on cells. *Biochemical and Biophysical Research Communications, 298*(1), 95-102.

Physical Activity and Health. (2011). Retrieved November 14, 2012, from http://www.cdc.gov/physicalactivity/everyone/health/index.html

Pipitone, N., & Scott, D. L. (2001). Magnetic pulse treatment for knee osteoarthritis: a randomised, double-blind, placebo-controlled study. *Curr Med Res Opin, 17*(3), 190-196.

Ramel, W., Goldin, P., Carmona, P., & McQuaid, J. (2004). The Effects of Mindfulness Meditation on Cognitive Processes and Affect in Patients with Past Depression. *Cognitive Therapy and Research, 28*(4), 433-455.

Reimers, C. D., Knapp, G., & Reimers, A. K. (2012). Does Physical Activity Increase Life Expectancy? A Review of the Literature. *Journal of Aging Research, 2012*, 9.

Richards, T. L., Lappin, M. S., Acosta-Urquidi, J., Kraft, G. H., Heide, A. C., Lawrie, F. W., et al. (1997). Double-blind study of pulsing magnetic field effects on multiple sclerosis. *J Altern Complement Med, 3*(1), 21-29.

Saeed, S. A., Antonacci, D. J., & Bloch, R. M. (2010). Exercise, yoga, and meditation for depressive and anxiety disorders. *American family physician, 81*(8), 981-986.

Sait, M. L., Wood, A. W., & Sadafi, H. A. (1999). A study of heart rate and heart rate variability in human subjects exposed to occupational levels of 50 Hz circularly polarised magnetic fields. *Medical Engineering & Physics, 21*(5), 361-369.

Sastre, A., Cook, M. R., & Graham, C. (1998). Nocturnal exposure to intermittent 60 Hz magnetic fields alters human cardiac rhythm. *Bioelectromagnetics, 19*(2), 98-106.

Schmid, M. R., Murbach, M., Lustenberger, C., Maire, M., Kuster, N., Achermann, P., et al. (2012). Sleep EEG alterations: effects of pulsed magnetic fields versus pulse-modulated radio frequency electromagnetic fields. *Journal of Sleep Research*, no-no.

Schneider, R. H., Grim, C. E., Rainforth, M. V., Kotchen, T., Nidich, S. I., Gaylord-King, C., et al. (2012). Stress Reduction in the Secondary Prevention of Cardiovascular Disease: Randomized, Controlled Trial of Transcendental Meditation and Health Education in Blacks. *Circulation: Cardiovascular Quality and Outcomes, 5*(6), 750-758.

Seyhan, N., & Canseven, A. G. (2006). In vivo effects of ELF MFs on collagen synthesis, free radical processes, natural antioxidant system, respiratory burst system, immune system activities, and electrolytes in the skin, plasma, spleen, lung, kidney, and brain tissues. *Electromagnetic Biology & Medicine, 25*(4), 291-305.

Sharrard, W. (1990). A double-blind trial of pulsed electromagnetic fields for delayed union of tibial fractures. *Journal of Bone & Joint Surgery, British Volume, 72-B*(3), 347-355.

Sherrill, D. L., Kotchou, K., & Quan, S. F. (1998). Association of physical activity and human sleep disorders. *Arch Intern Med, 158*(17), 1894-1898.

Shupak, N. M., McKay, J. C., Nielson, W. R., Rollman, G. B., Prato, F. S., & Thomas, A. W. (2006). Exposure to a specific pulsed low-frequency magnetic field: a double-blind placebo-controlled study of effects on pain ratings in rheumatoid arthritis and fibromyalgia patients. *Pain Res Manag, 11*(2), 85-90.

Stiller, M. J., Pak, G. H., Shupack, J. L., Thaler, S., Kenny, C., & Jondreau, L. (1992). A portable pulsed electromagnetic field (PEMF) device to enhance healing of recalcitrant venous ulcers: a double-blind, placebo-controlled clinical trial. *British Journal of Dermatology, 127*(2), 147-154.

Sutbeyaz, S. T., Sezer, N., & Koseoglu, B. F. (2006). The effect of pulsed electromagnetic fields in the treatment of cervical osteoarthritis: a randomized, double-blind, sham-controlled trial. *Rheumatol Int, 26*(4), 320-324.

Sutbeyaz, S. T., Sezer, N., Koseoglu, F., & Kibar, S. (2009). Low-frequency pulsed electromagnetic field therapy in fibromyalgia: a randomized, double-blind, sham-controlled clinical study. *Clin J Pain, 25*(8), 722-728.

Tribole, E., & Resch, E. (2012). *Intuitive Eating. A Revolutionary Program That Works*. New York: St. Martin's Press.

Trock, D. H., Bollet, A. J., & Markoll, R. (1994). The effect of pulsed electromagnetic fields in the treatment of osteoarthritis of the knee and cervical spine. Report of randomized, double blind, placebo controlled trials. *J Rheumatol, 21*(10), 1903-1911.

Uhlemann, C., Heinig, B., & Wollina, U. (2003). Therapeutic Ultrasound in Lower Extremity Wound Management. *The International Journal of Lower Extremity Wounds, 2*(3), 152-157.

Uzunca, K., Birtane, M., & Tastekin, N. (2007). Effectiveness of pulsed electromagnetic field therapy in lateral epicondylitis. *Clin Rheumatol, 26*(1), 69-74.

Varani, K., Gessi, S., Merighi, S., Iannotta, V., Cattabriga, E., Spisani, S., et al. (2002). Effect of low frequency electromagnetic fields on A2A adenosine receptors in human neutrophils. *British Journal of Pharmacology, 136*(1), 57-66.

vinh quôc Luong, K., & Thi Hoàng Nguyên, L. (2012). Vitamin D and Parkinson's disease. *Journal of Neuroscience Research, 90*(12), 2227-2236.

Volkow Nd, T. D. W. G., & et al. (2011). EFfects of cell phone radiofrequency signal exposure on brain glucose metabolism. *JAMA, 305*(8), 808-813.

Walker, J. (1983). Relief from chronic pain by low power laser irradiation. *Neuroscience Letters, 43*(2-3), 339-344.

Warden, S. J., Fuchs, R. K., Kessler, C. K., Avin, K. G., Cardinal, R. E., & Stewart, R. L. (2006). Ultrasound Produced by a

Conventional Therapeutic Ultrasound Unit Accelerates Fracture Repair. *Physical Therapy, 86*(8), 1118-1127.

Weinstock-Guttman, B., Mehta, B. K., Ramanathan, M., Karmon, Y., Henson, L. J., Halper, J., et al. (2012). Vitamin D and Multiple Sclerosis. *The Neurologist, 18*(4), 179-183 110.1097/NRL.1090b1013e31825bbf31835.

Weintraub, M. I., Wolfe, G. I., Barohn, R. A., Cole, S. P., Parry, G. J., Hayat, G., et al. (2003). Static magnetic field therapy for symptomatic diabetic neuropathy: a randomized, double-blind, placebo-controlled trial1 1 No commercial party having a direct financial interest in the results of the research supporting this article has or will confer a benefit upon the author(s) or upon any organization with which the author(s) is/are associated. *Archives of physical medicine and rehabilitation, 84*(5), 736-746.

Will, U., & Berg, E. (2007). Brain wave synchronization and entrainment to periodic acoustic stimuli. *Neuroscience Letters, 424*(1), 55-60.

Winker, R., Ivancsits, S., Pilger, A., Adlkofer, F., & Rudiger, H. W. (2005). Chromosomal damage in human diploid fibroblasts by intermittent exposure to extremely low-frequency electromagnetic fields. *Mutation Research, 585*(1-2), 43-49.

Wolf, F. I., Torsello, A., Tedesco, B., Fasanella, S., Boninsegna, A., D'Ascenzo, M., et al. (2005). 50-Hz extremely low frequency electromagnetic fields enhance cell proliferation and DNA damage: possible involvement of a redox mechanism. *Biochimica et Biophysica Acta, 1743*(1-2), 120-129.

Wolsko, P. M., Eisenberg, D. M., Simon, L. S., Davis, R. B., Walleczek, J., Mayo-Smith, M., et al. (2004). Double-blind placebo-controlled trial of static magnets for the treatment of osteoarthritis of the knee: results of a pilot study. *Alternative therapies in health and medicine, 10*(2), 36-43.

Woo, D. K., & Eide, M. J. (2010). Tanning beds, skin cancer, and vitamin D: an examination of the scientific evidence and public health implications. *Dermatologic Therapy, 23*(1), 61-71.

Yoo, M., Cho, Y., Kim, K., Chun, Y., & Chung, C. (2004). PULSED ELECTROMAGNETIC FIELDS TREATMENT FOR THE EARLY STAGES OF OSTEONECROSIS OF THE FEMORAL HEAD. *Journal of Bone & Joint Surgery, British Volume, 86-B*(SUPP II), 148-149.

Zittermann, A. (2006). Vitamin D and disease prevention with special reference to cardiovascular disease. *Progress in Biophysics and Molecular Biology, 92*(1), 39-48.

INDEX

A

Albert Einstein 171
alcohol 42, 61, 192, 199, 200
Alpha waves 33
amino acids 190, 191
amplitude xi, 12, 13, 14, 19, 22, 27, 48, 70, 73, 114, 123, 171, 202, 203, 206, 219, 223, 233
Amplitude xxiv, 13
antioxidant 17, 95, 104, 108, 193, 194, 235, 262
antioxidants 17, 102, 108, 189, 190, 191, 200
anxiety 73, 131, 133, 171, 199, 207, 215, 259, 260, 261
appliances 34, 81, 86, 88, 89, 90, 91, 104, 106, 109, 223, 228, 243, 244
atom 16, 17, 241
atoms 11, 16, 101, 102, 241
axons 22
Ayurveda 40, 77, 126
Ayurvedic 40, 76

B

Baby monitor 83, 90
baby monitors 25, 31, 84, 86, 91, 104, 106, 107, 228
balance 45, 70, 103, 114, 119, 121, 122, 123, 130, 162, 217, 223, 224, 226
Base Frequency xi, xix, xx, xxi, xxiii, xxiv, 8, 13, 14, 18, 21, 28, 30, 32, 34, 37, 39, 42, 46, 48, 60, 61, 62, 63, 67, 72, 74, 75, 76, 79, 80, 81, 93, 102, 103, 109, 111, 113, 114, 115, 119, 121, 122, 123, 125, 126, 128, 130, 131, 132, 133, 134, 135, 139, 140, 148, 149, 157, 158, 162, 164, 166, 167, 168, 169, 170, 175, 176, 187, 190, 192, 197, 202, 203, 211, 215, 216, 217, 218, 221, 224, 227, 233, 235, 237, 251, 252
Beta waves 33
Big Wave Rider xi
Binaural beats 206, 207, 211
blood pressure 31, 113, 121, 122, 131, 132, 133, 154, 172, 173, 174, 183, 189, 194, 209, 218, 219, 240
BLUE xxiii, 44, 45, 46, 49, 71, 79, 117, 120, 160, 164, 215, 217
body language 48, 49, 68, 69, 70, 71, 72, 80, 103, 121, 139, 140, 141, 142, 144, 145, 148, 151, 153, 154, 155, 160, 165, 166
brain 22, 23, 24, 26, 27, 33, 96, 99, 100, 105, 133, 145, 176, 178, 189, 203, 204, 205, 207, 210, 227, 235, 256, 258, 259, 260, 262, 263

brain waves 22, 228
Buddhism 126, 127, 208
Building of a Wave xxi, 3

C

Caffeine 192
calcium 24, 26, 189, 246, 248
cancer xxi, 96, 99, 100, 101, 213, 235, 238, 253, 256, 264
carcinogenic 101, 238
Carl Jung 175
Case Study xxi, 78, 103, 159, 162, 179, 198, 241, 247
cell phone 81, 83, 85, 86, 87, 91, 99, 100, 101, 106, 238, 259, 263
cellular phones 31
cellular telephone 31
cellular telephones 25, 86, 91
chlorine 25, 246
Christian 126
Chronic exposure 97
color 15, 30, 42, 46, 158, 162, 167, 168, 190, 192, 221, 225, 227, 228, 229, 233, 234, 237, 238
communication 25, 28, 31, 39, 77, 81, 82, 86, 87, 99, 177, 258
conditions xxi, 61, 100, 172, 204, 240, 243, 244, 249, 250
Constructive Interference xxiv, 13, 14, 29, 30, 251
cordless phones 25, 31, 83, 84, 85, 86, 91, 105, 107
Correlation 96, 99
cosmic radiation 88
cycle 13, 61, 114, 119, 123, 216, 235

D

depression 4, 103, 132, 133, 195, 215, 218, 259

Destructive Interference xxiv, 13, 14, 29, 30
diagnosis 76, 77, 210, 247
Discover xx, 37
disease ix, xxi, 17, 18, 42, 63, 74, 80, 94, 97, 98, 99, 101, 102, 108, 114, 123, 130, 132, 140, 191, 193, 194, 195, 198, 204, 210, 213, 214, 224, 233, 244, 247, 249, 251, 254, 257, 258, 261, 263, 265
diseases ix, x, xxi, 26, 100, 101, 194, 236, 238
Dissecting a Wave xxi, 9
dissertation ix
DNA 17, 95, 96, 97, 98, 102, 188, 190, 238, 246, 258, 264
doshas 40, 76
Dr. Brett Says xxi, 10, 14, 17, 24, 31, 34, 62, 74, 76, 77, 86, 87, 99, 107, 114, 133, 140, 158, 165, 166, 173, 176, 189, 197, 203, 210, 224, 236, 249

E

Ekahi x, xi, xix, xx, xxiii, xxiv, 8, 9, 10, 13, 14, 17, 18, 21, 25, 26, 28, 30, 34, 39, 40, 41, 44, 69, 76, 102, 109, 114, 125, 126, 128, 131, 133, 139, 141, 151, 152, 153, 154, 157, 161, 166, 171, 187, 192, 195, 196, 197, 198, 199, 202, 213, 215, 218, 224, 229, 234, 247, 251, 252
Ekahi Health Consultants 17
Ekahi Method x, xi, xix, xx, xxiii, xxiv, 8, 9, 10, 13, 14, 18, 21, 25, 26, 28, 30, 34, 39, 40, 41, 44, 69, 102, 109, 114, 125, 126, 128, 131, 133, 139, 141, 151,

152, 153, 154, 157, 161, 166,
171, 187, 192, 195, 196, 197,
198, 199, 202, 213, 215, 224,
229, 234, 247, 251, 252
electrical charges 25
electromagnetic x, 3, 9, 10, 11, 12, 13,
14, 15, 16, 18, 19, 21, 22, 24,
27, 28, 31, 32, 34, 81, 82, 83,
85, 86, 93, 105, 125, 224, 233,
238, 239, 240, 241, 243, 244,
251, 253, 254, 255, 256, 257,
258, 259, 261, 262, 263, 264
electromagnetic field 24, 244
electromagnetic radiation x, 9, 10, 11,
15, 27, 28, 32, 82, 85, 86, 93,
125, 240, 241, 243
Electromagnetic Spectrum 11, 15, 82
electrons 16, 94
Electrosmog 18, 32, 60, 63, 81, 83, 85,
88, 91, 93, 94, 102, 103, 113,
115, 123, 125, 221, 227, 251
ELF 18, 24, 26, 27, 31, 32, 81, 82,
85, 86, 87, 88, 90, 91, 93, 94,
95, 96, 97, 98, 99, 100, 101,
102, 103, 104, 105, 106, 107,
108, 109, 125, 227, 228, 243,
244, 255, 262
Emotional 46, 48, 260
energies ix, x, 14, 27, 46, 68, 159, 251
energy x, xix, xx, xxiii, xxiv, 8, 13, 14,
16, 19, 22, 27, 28, 30, 34, 39, 41,
42, 44, 47, 48, 49, 60, 61, 63,
68, 71, 72, 73, 74, 76, 81, 87,
88, 98, 101, 102, 114, 115, 116,
117, 118, 119, 122, 123, 127,
129, 134, 140, 149, 151, 156,
157, 159, 160, 165, 167, 171,
177, 183, 187, 188, 191, 192,
202, 204, 205, 208, 209, 211,
215, 224, 228, 229, 233, 234,
240, 241, 246, 247, 251, 252

environment 8, 18, 19, 30, 31, 63, 68,
83, 85, 86, 88, 104, 115, 120,
122, 125, 134, 139, 141, 171,
187, 188, 195, 199, 221, 223,
224, 225, 226, 227, 228, 229,
234, 235, 243, 251
environments x, 14, 17, 19, 30, 45, 60,
122, 168, 171, 202, 229
Enzymes 188
etiology ix
exercise x, xix, 19, 45, 61, 72, 76, 103,
104, 121, 144, 145, 147, 159,
163, 178, 180, 181, 187, 198,
199, 203, 205, 213, 214, 215,
216, 217, 218, 219, 220, 222,
223, 234, 242, 251
eye contact 48, 70, 71, 72, 73, 140,
141, 144, 145, 148, 151, 153,
154, 155, 160

F

Faraday 82
Fats 191
Feng Shui 221, 224, 228
fibromyalgia ix, 79, 245, 262, 263
Flow 225, 226
food 19, 21, 45, 48, 61, 85, 105, 187,
188, 190, 195, 196, 197, 198,
199, 200, 213, 251
food sensitivities 45, 48, 197, 198
forces 8, 10, 11, 125, 242
free radical 16, 17, 96, 98, 101, 102,
108, 189, 235, 262
free radicals 16, 17, 18, 101, 102, 194,
235
Free radical theory 98
frequencies x, xxiv, 9, 11, 13, 14, 15,
18, 19, 22, 23, 27, 28, 29, 30, 31,
32, 33, 34, 39, 48, 63, 67, 68, 70,
73, 74, 75, 81, 82, 83, 84, 85,

86, 88, 91, 93, 98, 102, 114, 115, 122, 123, 125, 134, 141, 149, 165, 187, 190, 203, 205, 206, 207, 238, 240, 246, 248, 251
frequency x, xix, xxiii, 11, 12, 16, 18, 19, 22, 23, 24, 25, 26, 27, 28, 31, 33, 39, 40, 41, 46, 60, 63, 67, 68, 69, 70, 71, 72, 73, 74, 75, 77, 79, 81, 82, 84, 87, 88, 101, 103, 106, 113, 114, 115, 122, 125, 139, 140, 146, 149, 150, 151, 153, 157, 158, 159, 160, 162, 164, 165, 166, 167, 168, 169, 171, 175, 187, 188, 191, 201, 202, 203, 206, 207, 208, 213, 215, 216, 217, 219, 221, 223, 233, 234, 237, 238, 239, 240, 241, 243, 244, 246, 248, 251, 252, 255, 258, 259, 262, 263, 264
Frequency xi, xii, xx, xxi, xxiii, xxiv, 12, 30, 34, 39, 40, 41, 43, 44, 46, 61, 62, 63, 67, 69, 70, 71, 72, 73, 74, 76, 78, 79, 80, 83, 87, 88, 89, 91, 94, 102, 103, 113, 114, 115, 116, 117, 118, 121, 122, 125, 126, 128, 131, 133, 137, 139, 140, 141, 148, 149, 150, 151, 153, 154, 155, 156, 157, 158, 159, 160, 161, 162, 164, 165, 167, 168, 169, 171, 187, 199, 201, 202, 213, 215, 217, 219, 220, 221, 224, 243, 251, 256, 258, 259
Frequency Tuning xxiv, 139, 140, 148, 149, 150, 151, 153, 154, 155, 156, 157, 160, 161, 162, 169
Fruits 189

G

Gamma waves 33
geomagnetic 88
gravity 10
GREEN xxiii, 44, 45, 46, 48, 70, 76, 79, 103, 117, 120, 121, 151, 215, 217
Guided Visualizations 127

H

happiness xix, 7, 8, 30, 166, 173, 174, 175
Hawaii 3, 4, 8
heal x, 8
healing xxi, 6, 7, 22, 127, 206, 219, 241, 242, 243, 244, 246, 248, 249, 250, 252, 262
Healing with Waves xxi
health xix, xx, 18, 30, 40, 41, 42, 67, 74, 75, 76, 77, 79, 81, 82, 91, 93, 94, 96, 97, 99, 101, 102, 103, 104, 119, 123, 125, 127, 134, 135, 139, 152, 154, 155, 163, 179, 189, 190, 191, 192, 193, 210, 213, 214, 216, 224, 227, 228, 235, 242, 243, 244, 246, 249, 255, 256, 258, 261, 264
healthy x, 67, 74, 76, 77, 103, 120, 130, 159, 191, 196, 200, 204, 216, 221, 234, 256
heart xxiii, 21, 26, 27, 31, 40, 41, 42, 46, 72, 73, 75, 78, 102, 103, 109, 129, 131, 145, 161, 172, 173, 174, 175, 179, 183, 189, 191, 194, 195, 209, 213, 214, 233, 240, 257, 258, 261
heart rate 26, 41, 42, 46, 72, 73, 75, 78, 102, 103, 109, 131, 145, 161, 172, 173, 174, 175, 183, 189, 209, 214, 234, 261
heat x, 15, 27, 30, 45, 75, 87, 191, 238, 239, 240, 248
Hertz xxiv, 12, 23, 27, 82, 248
hormones 98, 189, 215, 235
hypertension 26, 213

I

IARC 101
ICNIRP 89, 106
Important Point xxi, 15, 17, 18, 23, 24, 27, 42, 60, 97, 115, 141, 150, 156
Infrared 10, 27, 30, 75, 83, 233, 238, 239, 240, 242, 243, 260
infrared radiation 15, 27, 75, 224, 238
interact 10, 15, 19, 34, 88, 159, 224, 251
intuition 168, 171, 175, 176, 177, 178, 180, 181, 187, 195, 196, 198, 199, 210, 251
In-vitro 94, 95, 96
In-vivo 94, 95, 96, 100
ion 24, 25, 34, 102, 248
ionizing 14, 15, 16, 18, 19, 21, 27, 28, 30, 32, 34, 75, 80, 81, 82, 84, 85, 91, 97, 98, 99, 238, 240
ions 24, 25, 26, 97, 98, 246
Ion Theory 97

J

Judaism 126

K

Kundalini 127

L

Laser 241, 253, 256, 258
lightning 32, 88, 243

M

magnetic field ix, 18, 22, 24, 28, 31, 34, 82, 86, 89, 90, 94, 96, 97, 104, 244, 246, 254, 255, 261, 262, 264
Magnetic fields 88

Magnetic Induction Theory 98
magnetite 31
Maharishi Mahesh Yogi 126
mantra 126, 127, 129, 130, 208, 211
Marconi 82
Master the Waves of Life x, xix, xxi, 8, 21, 46, 74, 78, 251, 252
Match 141, 145
matter x, 10, 13, 14, 27, 28, 105, 146, 149, 152, 154, 164, 165, 187, 258, 260
Maxwell 82
mechanical 3, 9, 10, 12, 13, 14, 18, 19, 21, 28, 30, 224, 248, 251
medicine 40, 77, 126, 187, 258, 264
meditation 3, 4, 8, 22, 79, 122, 125, 126, 128, 129, 130, 131, 132, 133, 134, 135, 199, 206, 207, 208, 211, 219, 251, 252, 259, 260, 261
Meditation Beads 126
meditations 4, 126, 127, 129, 208
melatonin 83, 98, 104, 194, 195, 235, 236, 237, 242, 253
Melatonin 108, 194, 235, 236, 255
membranes 24, 98, 246
Mental 46, 48
Metabolism 45, 46
microwave 9, 31, 81, 84, 86, 106, 227, 239, 257
Microwave oven 83, 105
Microwaves 10
Mindfulness 127, 255, 258, 261
modalities 249, 250
molecule 17, 101
molecules 16, 17, 31, 101, 102, 191, 248
Mozart 223
multiple sclerosis ix, 253, 255, 261
music 14, 30, 86, 147, 160, 187, 201, 202, 203, 204, 205, 206, 208, 211, 213, 221, 223, 226, 234, 251, 260, 261
Music 201, 202, 226

N

natural xxiii
Natural Zone xxiii, xxiv, 8, 14, 19, 47, 61, 62, 63, 67, 74, 114, 115, 119, 121, 132, 133, 159, 160, 164, 165, 169, 175, 183, 200, 203, 205, 210, 228, 229, 251
nerve 25, 26, 189, 249, 250
neurons 25
new age 4
non-ionizing radiation 16, 18, 27, 28, 30
nonionizing radiation 238
nourish 30, 34, 61, 190, 213, 216, 217
Nourish With Resonant Frequencies xxi, 251

O

objective xxiii, 39, 40, 41, 75, 141, 199
ocean 3, 7, 9, 14, 172
Om 129, 208
One xix, 3, 10, 14, 21, 22, 27, 34, 108, 149, 190, 203, 214, 238, 251, 255
overhead power lines 88, 89, 91, 94

P

PEMF 244, 245, 246, 247, 249, 252, 253, 262
PhD iii, ix
photons 27, 28, 233, 234, 241
Physical 3, 4, 7, 46, 48, 120, 121, 148, 213, 214, 246, 254, 260, 261, 264
Physical Therapist 3, 4, 7, 246
physiotherapist ix
pineal gland 31, 83, 194, 235, 236, 237
pitch 141, 145, 146, 147, 151, 173, 202
positive effects xix, 97, 99, 193, 214

potassium 24, 25, 189, 246
preventing xxi, 193
profile xxiii, 39, 41
Profile xii, 39, 40, 41, 43, 44, 46, 67, 73, 76, 79, 102, 121, 128, 133, 159, 162, 164, 199, 217, 219, 251
proteins 98, 102, 188, 189, 190, 191, 193, 196, 199
pulsed 93, 103, 253, 255, 258, 259, 262, 263

Q

Qi Gong 127, 130

R

radiation x, 10, 11, 14, 15, 16, 18, 19, 24, 27, 28, 30, 32, 34, 75, 80, 81, 82, 83, 84, 85, 86, 88, 99, 224, 237, 238, 239, 240, 241, 243, 257, 259
radio waves x, 18, 31
RED xxiii, 44, 45, 46, 48, 69, 70, 76, 79, 115, 120, 121, 133, 139, 158, 167, 216, 217, 219
Research 33, 78, 94, 95, 101, 108, 131, 132, 171, 195, 207, 213, 235, 236, 244, 249, 253, 254, 258, 259, 260, 261, 262, 263, 264
Reset xxi, 30, 61, 74, 79, 103, 111, 123, 126, 130, 131, 133, 140, 148, 162, 164, 168, 224, 251
Resonance xxiv, 165, 201
resonant 19, 122, 151, 169, 251
resonate x, 30, 130, 160, 167, 169, 177, 183, 187, 190, 251
respiratory rate xxiii, 40, 41, 43, 46, 73
resting heart rate xxiii, 26, 40, 46
ride the waves x, 8

S

SAD 236, 242, 243
Sanskrit 40, 126, 129, 208
SAR 85, 87, 91, 106, 107
Schumann 32, 33, 34, 244, 246
Schumann Resonances 32, 33, 34
seasonal affective disorder (SAD) 236
Self-hypnosis 127
Sense External Frequencies xx, 65
sleep 22, 33, 40, 44, 48, 49, 76, 83, 104, 106, 107, 108, 115, 120, 121, 122, 199, 204, 206, 207, 214, 221, 226, 228, 235, 236, 237, 254, 262
Sleep 44, 46, 48, 120, 121, 221, 262
Smart meters 83
smells 221, 223, 227, 229
Social 46, 48, 120, 121
sodium 24, 25, 189, 246
Sound 10, 21
sounds xix, 19, 28, 30, 63, 68, 130, 146, 207, 213, 222, 223, 226, 248
spinal cord 22, 189, 191
spiritual 4, 5, 7, 8, 126, 216
static magnets 247, 256, 258, 264
stress 73, 76, 114, 134, 172, 173, 174, 175, 199, 207, 259
strong forces 10
subtle signs 68, 77
success xix, xx, 46, 155, 160
successful xix, xx, 4, 67, 74, 134, 141, 153, 155, 158, 162, 163, 167, 169, 181
summate xxiv, 13, 19, 34, 74, 85, 165, 251
sun x, 11, 15, 27, 28, 31, 83, 88, 222, 234, 235, 236, 237, 238, 243
Superstring theory 10
symptoms 40, 79, 103, 114, 122, 131, 133, 134, 172, 173, 198, 199, 210, 215, 241, 252, 258

T

Tai Chi 45, 127, 130
Taoism 126
temperature 27, 48, 70, 76, 77, 154, 215, 216, 221
Tesla 82, 89, 149
The Frequency Profile xxiii, 39, 41
Theta waves 207
tissue 22, 25, 31, 85, 87, 91, 96, 133, 189, 241, 243, 248, 256
Torah 126
Transcendental meditation 126
Transformers 106, 228
treatments xxi, 133, 246
Tune Frequency for Success xxi, 137

U

UHF 25, 81, 83, 85, 86, 87, 91, 93, 94, 96, 98, 99, 100, 101, 102, 103, 104, 105, 106, 107, 108, 109, 125, 227, 228
ultrasound 248, 249, 250, 256
Ultrasound 10, 248, 249, 257, 259, 260, 263
Ultraviolet 10, 16, 83, 233, 237, 240, 242
unhappiness 3

V

Vedas 40, 126
vegetables 188, 189, 190, 192, 193, 196, 200, 219
vibration 147, 149, 173, 176, 177, 178, 196, 198, 199, 208, 251
VIOLET xxiii, 44, 45, 46, 49, 71, 76, 103, 118, 121, 149, 158, 167, 217
visible light 15, 18, 27, 28, 34, 75, 83, 233, 238

Visible light 10
Vitamin D 193, 194, 236, 237, 253, 255, 257, 259, 263, 264, 265
vitamins 189, 190, 191
Vitamins 189
Voltage-gated channel theory 98

W

water 10, 14, 31, 60, 101, 188, 191, 195, 200, 219, 222, 224, 226
watts 85, 87
wave xi, xii, xx, xxiii, xxiv, 8, 9, 12, 13, 14, 16, 18, 19, 21, 22, 23, 24, 25, 33, 60, 61, 62, 63, 67, 74, 87, 96, 114, 132, 133, 140, 158, 159, 160, 162, 165, 167, 169, 170, 197, 202, 206, 207, 208, 210, 215, 228, 233, 240, 248, 251, 264
Wave Amplifier xxiii, xxiv, 29, 192, 203
wavelength x, 12, 30, 233, 241
Wave Reducers xxiv, 14, 19, 28, 30, 34, 47, 60, 61, 62, 63, 114, 115, 123, 125, 198, 199, 200, 205, 210, 211, 251
waves x, xi, xix, xx, xxi, xxiii, xxiv, 3, 7, 8, 9, 10, 11, 12, 13, 14, 15, 18, 19, 21, 22, 23, 24, 25, 26, 27, 28, 29, 30, 31, 33, 34, 46, 60, 61, 62, 74, 75, 80, 81, 82, 83, 86, 88, 91, 94, 96, 98, 102, 103, 105, 113, 114, 119, 123, 126, 165, 169, 187, 202, 206, 207, 222, 224, 227, 229, 233, 239, 241, 243, 248, 251, 252
Waves x, xix, xxi, 3, 8, 10, 12, 14, 19, 21, 46, 74, 78, 224, 231, 233, 248, 251, 252
weak forces 10

Wi-Fi 82, 84
wireless x, 25, 26, 31, 81, 82, 83, 84, 85, 86, 87, 88, 91, 94, 98, 103, 104, 105, 107, 109, 258
Wireless router 83, 107
wireless routers 25, 31, 84, 86, 91, 99
wiring 24, 34, 86, 88, 91, 94, 104, 243, 244
World Health Organization 95, 96, 256

X

X-rays 10, 18, 76, 240

Y

YELLOW xi, xxiii, 44, 45, 46, 48, 69, 70, 116, 120, 159, 160, 162, 163, 167, 217

Z

Zazen 127, 128

ABOUT THE AUTHOR

Brett Wade, PhD

Brett Wade graduated *summa cum laude* from the University of Medicine and Dentistry of New Jersey (Rutgers) with a doctorate in Health Sciences. His research examined health effects related to fluctuations in the earth's magnetic field. He also has a bachelor's degree and a master's degree in Physical Therapy.

Throughout his career as a physical therapist, Brett was fascinated with the therapeutic effects of pulsed electromagnetic fields in treating disease; this eventually became the impetus for his doctorate work. Brett also started to wonder if the electromagnetic fields produced by humans were perceptible by other humans and whether they affected our relationships and our health.

While living in Hawaii, Brett began to develop the idea that the one thing that connects all living and nonliving things is invisible waves. Years later, he developed the frequency profile to assign people into one of the five base frequencies. Thus, the Ekahi Method was born (*ekahi* meaning "one" in Hawaiian).

Currently, Brett lectures full-time at Okanagan College in Kelowna, B.C. (Canada), and he regularly speaks about the Ekahi Method. Book Brett for a speaking engagement at www.ekahimethod.com.